HAPPINESS AFTER 30:

THE PARADOX OF AGING

DR JOLANTA BURKE

JUMPP

Published in Ireland by
JUMPP PUBLISHING
Clonsilla · Dublin 15 · Ireland

Copyright © 2017 Dr Jolanta Burke www.drjolantaburke.com

First published in 2016

Cover designed by © 2016 Artur Bukowski
Typeset by Anna Zalewska-Szczech

ISBN: 978-1-910998-02-1

TABLE OF CONTENTS

ABOUT THE AUTHOR

Jolanta Burke, PhD, is a psychologist specialising in Positive Psychology. She received her PhD from Trinity College Dublin and is currently a Senior Lecturer and an Associate Leader of the Masters in Applied Positive Psychology and Coaching Psychology programme at the University of East London,. She loves working with students and seeing them grow. She supervises their work in a wide range of Positive Psychology-related areas.

Jolanta is passionate about Positive Psychology and her mission in life is to help people understand and use it effectively in their lives. She appears regularly in the media, writes extensively for both magazines and newspapers, such as the Guardian and the Irish Independent, and frequently speaks on radio and at various events around the world. A few years ago, she hosted a popular weekly radio programme about evidence-based well-being, and was acknowledged by The Irish Times as one of 30 people who make Ireland happier.

Jolanta lives with her husband Brendan, step-son Charlie, friendly dog Rosie, and shy cat Freddie in suburban Dublin. To find out more about her, please visit www.drjolantaburke.com; and follow her on Facebook, Twitter @jolantaburke. Please check out Jolanta's YouTube channel: Positive Psychology for Life with Dr Jolanta Burke, for free videos on Positive Psychology.

To my mum and Bren.
Love you always.

Special thanks to Ania, Gracey and Artur
for all your help.

THE WOMAN WHO CHANGED IT ALL

When she walked into the auditorium, the entire room went quiet. She was a guest lecturer from Harvard, whose presentation we had all looked forward to for months. We were in our first year of Masters in Applied Positive Psychology, and just like sponges, we soaked in vast amounts of knowledge from every lecture we attended, processed it fast, and then made a judgement as to the usefulness of what we had learnt. Some lectures left me astounded, others inquisitive, yet this lecture changed my life forever.

Curiously, it is not the main topic she presented that remained with me for years, rather a flippant comment she made about a natural change that occurs in the level of happiness over our lifespan. When I got back home, I could not stop thinking about it. I stayed up late that night searching for empirical evidence behind her statement, and reasons as to why that change occurs.

Today, a decade later, I have some of my questions answered, however, the more I read about this topic the more questions I seem to have. Nonetheless, I hope to share some of these findings with you, so that, hopefully, they can change the way you look at happiness and help you feel better on days, weeks, months, and years when things are just not going so well for you. I hope that what you read in this book will change your life, just as it has changed mine.

The pursuit of happiness

If you are unhappy it is all your fault – this is what the media continuously tries to make us believe.

This outrageous message is driven by the gigantic vehicle that is the self-help industry, which has taken control of many aspects of our lives. A survey carried out in the UK and the US reported that between six and nine out of 10 mental health professionals recommend self-help resources to their clients[1]. Going for therapy, nowadays, is apparently not enough. Even therapists encourage us to read self-help books. With ever growing demand, the self-help industry continues to flourish.

In 1998, approximately 3,700 American book titles began with the words *How to*[2]; by 2008, self-help became the top selling genre[3] and remains there to this day[4]. Despite this, our levels of well-being have plummeted and depression rates are worryingly high, making us want to read the *How to* books even more. There are thousands of titles in the self-help section, which vary from *How to*: …stop worrying; …think more about sex; …get a girlfriend; …dump a girlfriend; …get my girlfriend to lose weight; or …*find your (first) husband.* These are all authentic titles!

One of the most appealing *How to* series, however, relates to happiness. After all, if you were to ask people what they truly want in life, the majority of us would probably say happiness. Happiness is like a saffron thread, so precious and hard to get, which is why books about it seem to pop up faster than mushrooms in my back garden. I live in wet-soiled Ireland, so it is a particularly bold statement.

Apart from happiness books, we watch movies that perpetuate the myths of happiness, such as *Eat, Pray, Love*; *Wild*; *Hector and the Search for Happiness*; *The Secret Life of Walter Mitty*; or *The Way*. They all make us believe that if we feel unhappy, what we need to do is radically change our lives. Thus, we quit our relationships, jobs, or even our entire lives, and escape into the new, unknown, and what seems a more exciting life, hoping it will fix all our problems. Then, we realise that grass is not always greener on the other side, and once we change our perspective, we do not feel any happier at all.

One of the popular vehicles for boosting happiness is travelling. Escaping from our troubled lives has become a solution to many happiness-related problems. A gap year used to be for school leavers, or for twenty somethings who were either half-way through, or at the end of their formal education. The aim was to go out there, meet new people, and have an adventure of a lifetime before settling down to the nitty-gritty of daily life. However, trends are changing with the speed of light, and as of 2009, 30 to 55 year olds were twice as likely to take a year out to travel as people in their 20s[5]. They escape from the settled life, which has not worked for them so well, and hope that the break-away will either grace them with new life partners, fresh locations, where they can start over and put down new roots, yet again, or at least provide them with a breather from the doom and gloom of daily slog. Travel has thus become an escape from unhappiness.

If we cannot afford to travel, we escape our lives in other ways. Some of us withdraw from society and become loners. We secretly want something else, something that seems unattainable, which is why we stop trying to make any effort to change our lives and instead, pretend to be happy. Others, on the other hand, throw themselves into a manic pursuit of happiness by signing up to weekend retreats, practicing Positive Psychology activities[6], maybe even following some less evidence-based activities promising a better life.

A few weeks ago, I received an email from someone who attended a two-day Positive Psychology workshop, read three books about it, and inspired by his new knowledge, designed a six- week online course and a smartphone app, which you can buy for big bucks to boost your happiness. The ironic thing is that research reviewing online interventions found that some of them are not very good at improving our well-being[7]. More interestingly yet, some recent studies show that the pursuit of happiness may actually lead to increased levels of loneliness and lower well-being[8], which seems a little bit ironic.

I am not a naturally happy-clappy person. In many of the well-being questionnaires I completed over the years, I scored either average or below average in my well-being (depending on what was happening in my life at that time). I trusted the media message banging on about taking responsibility for our happiness: *If you are unhappy, it must be your fault,* so I chose to take action.

Being a hardworking person, who does not shy away from a challenge, feeling less happy made me pursue this ephemeral happiness even harder. Every time I felt a pang in the pit of my stomach that alerted me to a slight dip in my happiness levels, I would rise to the challenge and begin to exercise, meditate, count my blessings, socialise, use my character strengths, practice optimistic thinking and hopefulness, eat more wholesome foods, do something meaningful, volunteer, forgive those who I held a grudge against, play, spend more time with my partner, write a diary, listen to TED Talks, search the internet and academic journals for evidence-based interventions, and do other, crazy things to keep the happy feelings going.

My friends used to say that I was a shining example of how a person should live their life. As flattering as it was, I was very doubtful about the merits of their statement. Doing all these amazing things did make me feel better, but this happiness malarkey seemed damn hard work to do. That said, I did not want to hurt their feelings so I just smiled cheerfully and kept up with my psychological, sweat-provoking pursuit of something better, bigger, and bolder. Until that one day, when I heard the guest lecturer talk about happiness changing throughout our lifespan. That day, I realised that perhaps I was putting myself under a little bit too much pressure.

Happiness after 30

What the guest lecturer said was simple, yet profound. She claimed that there was strong evidence to suggest that happiness is not a stable characteristic, meaning that it is not like the colour of our eyes, which are blue, green, or brown for the rest of our lives. Regardless of how many happiness-boosting activities we do, what self-development courses we attend, or the number of countries we visit on our travels, our level of happiness fluctuates throughout our lifespan.

What was even more interesting is that, according to the speaker, women feel the least happy at the age of 37, and men at the age of 42. *So* – she reassured us – *if you are around this age, do not worry, things will get better!*

When I heard her say that, I was in my early 30s and already feeling the pressure of the new decade creeping up on me. She explained that once we reach our early 20s our happiness begins to drop, reaching the lowest point in our late 30s to early 40s, only to increase thereafter. This means that people at the age of 55 are more or less at the same level of happiness as those at the age of 20. And again, let me emphasize that it happens notwithstanding how much we engage in happiness-boosting activities.

What she said resonated with me, as I saw my friends going through hard times in their 30s and 40s. A friend of mine, Frieda, seemed to have it all: a lovely husband, two healthy boys, a job she enjoyed, a nice house, and a holiday twice a year, and to add to it all a nasty bout of debilitating depression. Another friend, who spent her 30s trying for a baby, remembered these times as some of the toughest of her life. Mid-40s became a tension-release, where she no longer had to try desperately to be a mum and felt more content with her lot.

At that time, my older friends, those in their 50s and 60s, seemed the happiest of all. They had the perspective that I, as well as some of my younger buddies, found hard to summon. They also had an abundance of hopefulness they generously shared, which helped me develop my optimism. This is why, what I heard that day in the auditorium began to make more and more sense to me, spiking my curiosity, so I wanted to know more.

I wanted to find out if this is just one researcher's opinion, or perhaps a common understanding among psychologists. I wanted to figure out what changes we go through in our 30s and 40s that make our happiness levels drop to such an extent; as well as what happens inside us that makes us happier thereafter. I hoped that my knowledge of these changes could help me speed up the process of recovery from the dip and turn my life around that little bit faster. After all, the sooner we learn how to drive the car, the faster we can get the licence. I wanted to get my licence, for living a good life, as soon as possible.

To do this, I reviewed some studies carried out in psychology and other fields that may shed light on the secret of U-shaped happiness. I also considered an array of models for happiness, well-being, and flourishing to identify what may be causing this dip. I searched for other, less known psychological theories, to see if they can help us understand the fall and rise in our happiness. Having read tons of research, I selected what I believe are the five natural changes that occur in us that can ultimately help us live a better life. So, buckle up and enjoy the ride. Let us discover why our happiness fluctuates throughout our lives, and what we can do to minimise the dip and keep the positivity thriving.

ROLLERCOASTER OF LIFE

For years, psychologists have not found much evidence of peaks and troughs in happiness throughout our lives. Many even rejected the idea of midlife crisis claiming it was just a myth[9] perpetuated by the media, which based their views on an opinion of one man: Elliot Jaques, a psychotherapist, who noticed that artists' creativity declined in their mid-years and blamed it on an existential wobble they experienced in their late 30s and 40s. This is why, it took a lot of persuasion for psychologists to believe that happiness may actually alter throughout our lifespan. One of the first series of studies that provided the evidence for it was carried out by economists[10], rather than psychologists.

Happiness in numbers

In 2008, two economists, Blanchflower and Oswald, analysed data of over half a million people across 50 countries[11]. Using various measures and comparing persons of different ages, as well as assessing them throughout many years of their lives, the researchers found that happiness is U-shaped. It measures high when we are in our 20s, then begins to drop, and plummets around midlife, only to go up again thereafter. Thus, by the time we reach 55, our happiness is more or less at the same level as those at the age of 20.

According to the above study, happiness reached its lowest level at different ages in various countries. For instance, we are at our lowest in the UK at the age of 35, in Ireland at the age of 38, and in the USA at the age of 44. Many follow up studies carried out by other researchers showed a similar trend[12]; even though the age of the peak and trough differs, it ranges between mid to late 30s to 50s. Mind you, some studies did not report a U-shaped happiness at all, but there were relatively fewer of those[13]. Thus, nowadays, psychologists are slowly beginning to believe that, indeed, we may be experiencing some changes in our happiness across the lifespan.

While a U-shaped happiness trend exists, many studies report different findings in relation to age and the depth of dip. This may be due to various factors. Firstly, there are political and social policy differences between the countries measured, which affect the results[14]. Also, the sample of participants who were used in the studies were different. Sometimes they were randomly selected; other times they were sourced through various organisations, which may have influenced their responses. Yet another reason for their differences is due to the questionnaires that were used to measure happiness, of which there are many. Even though all of them report *happiness*, the way they measure it is different. Let us delve deeper into this conundrum.

Measuring stick

Ireland is part of the European Union, and as such, uses a metric system. Before we joined the Union, and for many years thereafter, we had an imperial system. Then, one day, it all began to change. The transition was difficult for most of us. For instance, we drove our cars, which indicated miles, on roads that showed us speed limits in kilometres. In order to avoid speeding and being stopped by the police, we needed to quickly calculate in our heads the speed limit for each stretch of road and compare it with our own speed readings in the car. As challenging as it seems, it was doable because we can easily convert metric measures into imperial and vice versa. We have a simple measuring stick that allows us to do it. If only happiness were that simple.

As it stands, we have many theories of happiness, and even more models of well-being and flourishing. Unfortunately, unlike the metric and imperial systems, we do not have a measuring stick that could easily compare one theory with the other, which may be the reason why we have such varied results across age in relation to happiness.

Each of the theories of well-being consists of certain components, such as experiences of positive emotions, or meaning in life. Some of them overlap across different theories, others do not. The psychologists who create these theories base them on either previous research carried out by other researchers or provide their own research findings. Either way, they argue in an academic paper why their theory is the most applicable for measuring happiness, and if their argument is solid, or if they are famous psychologists, their ideas are taken on board and the theory is then used by other researchers to measure well-being.

It is a similar process to a talent show on TV. Three friends watch it together and comment on what they can see. One gives a more compelling argument than another, or is more influential in the group, thus the rest change their views based on her opinion. The difference between a talent show and well-being theories is that the latter are based on scientific evidence, rather than just psychologists' opinions of what theory is better, however a similar process of influence applies.

Components of well-being

You may have noticed that I differentiated between happiness, well-being, and flourishing. They are all conceptually different terms, as well as consisting of a range of, sometimes dissimilar, components. In order to better understand our happiness changes after 30, we need to briefly look at these differences.

When psychologists say happiness, we usually refer to *subjective well-being.* In the late 60s a student of psychology, Ed Diener, was curious about happiness and wanted to study it for his PhD. At that time, psychologists were influenced by Freud, according to whom the only promise we can make to our patients is to help them transform their "hysteric misery into common unhappiness"[15]. Freud did not believe that happiness existed, which says more about him than it does about his patients. Yet, other psychologists shared his views for years to come, claiming that our happiness level is set in stone, cannot be altered or measured, therefore there is no point in studying it and attempting to change it. This is possibly why Ed Diener's supervisor did not entertain his ideas, and so Ed had to give happiness up as a PhD research topic.

His supervisor's opinion did not, however, stop him from pursuing it further. After completing his PhD, he became a professor of psychology at the University of Illinois, where he began doing research trying to figure out what made people happy. One thing that he noticed was that every time he talked to his esteemed colleagues about happiness, their eyes glossed over. They found the term happiness too fluffy to take seriously and study, which is why he coined the term *subjective well-being* that is psychological lingo for happiness[16].

Research into *subjective well-being* shows us that what makes people happy are three things: 1. higher levels of experiencing positive emotions, 2. lower levels of experiencing negative emotions, and 3. being satisfied with our lives. This theory is very simple and has also become a foundation for, so called, hedonic happiness, which is experiencing well-being through life pleasures.

When we analyse changes of subjective well-being after 30, we see that indeed, there is evidence of it dropping in our late 30s or early 40s and increasing into the 50s and 60s, only to drop again after 75[17]. Therefore, many of the studies reporting U-shaped happiness assess well-being as hedonic happiness. They use very simple questionnaires that measure our experiences of pleasurable emotions and ask us different versions of the question: How satisfied are you with your lot? Based on participants' responses they see U-shaped changes after 30.

This theory, however, was heavily criticised by other psychologists who claimed that it is too simplistic. If happiness were indeed just about pleasure and life satisfaction, then it would not explain why some people experience what is commonly known as contentment, without actually feeling a burst of positive emotions. Let me illustrate what I mean.

One of my friends has gone through a really tough patch in life. In the space of six months, her mother became very ill and passed away. Whilst looking after her mum, she felt a mixture of emotions; a lot of sadness, anger, but also she experienced an odd sense of contentment. She was grateful that she had a chance to spend her mother's last days with her. In the six months of her mother's battle with cancer, she realised how precious life is and how easy it is to lose it all, so she felt blessed for the gift of life. After her mum's death, she floundered for a while, struggling to make sense of what had happened. However, soon she was able to see a meaning in all these tragic events and even talked about the benefits of her trauma. It allowed her to see the strength in herself she had never thought existed. Subsequently, she changed her life direction, went back to college to retrain herself, changed her job, and began to live her life to the full. Her life was not necessarily full of daily pleasures. Instead, she experienced a deeper feeling of contentment and appreciation of life. Her post traumatic growth made her happier in a different sort of way.

This type of happiness is sometimes referred to as *chaironic*[18], stemming from experiencing tragic events. However, the components of happiness that develop in us as a result of a challenging life journey can be viewed as similar to those of *psychological well-being*[19], otherwise referred to as *eudaimonic happiness*.

The concept of eudaimonia originates from Aristotle, according to whom, true happiness comes from realising our potential, by living virtuous lives, and doing what is worthwhile doing[20]. It is about developing self-acceptance, which refers to evaluating ourselves and our lives with kindness and understanding; experiencing personal growth, which is an ability to learn from various situations in life; having purpose in life, which is a goal that drives our daily actions; enjoying positive relations with others; having autonomy to do what we wish in our lives; and experiencing environmental mastery, which is a belief that we can get ourselves out of any situation we find ourselves in, by influencing our environment[21]. In short, *psychological well-being,* or *eudaimonic happiness,* is a more sophisticated type of happiness, which is described as contentment in everyday language.

There is very little research carried out about changes of *eudaimonic happiness* across our lifespan and there are inconsistencies in the findings that are available. For example, one study compared people aged 20, 50, and 75 and identified no differences between ages in relation to self-acceptance[22]. However, another study found that some age differences exist, because with age, we contextualise our lives better, which results in more self-acceptance[23]. This is why, when searching for differences in happiness after 30, I have also reviewed some of the individual components of eudaimonic happiness.

Apart from these two main models of happiness, we also have the whole range of other well-being models, such as *Five Essential Elements for Wellbeing* created by the *Gallup Organisation*[24], which consist of: career, social, financial, physical, and community well-being. Another theory was created in the *Foresight Report* by the *New Economic Foundation*, according to which there are five ways to experience well-being: 1. Connecting with people, 2. Being active, 3. Taking notice, otherwise known as savouring, 4. Keeping learning, and 5. Giving to others[25].

These are just a few examples of well-known theories, but there are many more that introduce different components of what is believed to be well-being. Some of these theories do not even have any components, as they are a component of well-being themselves. For instance, *halcyonic happiness,* which comes from living a serene life, full of acceptance for self and others; *prudential happiness,* that is experienced through flow and engagement; or previously-mentioned *chaironic happiness,* that comes from experiencing tragic circumstances, such as that which my friend experienced when her mother passed away[26].

Apart from all these different forms of happiness and an even wider range of theories on well-being, we also have a concept of *flourishing* that has sprung up in the last few years. *Flourishing* incorporates both *hedonic* and *eudaimonic happiness* and offers a more holistic view of our optimal functioning[27]. Some of their components are similar, such as positive relationships, and meaning and/or purpose; other elements are different across them, such as experiences of positive emotions, resilience, or self-esteem.

When researching for this book, I reviewed all the components across happiness, and other type of well-being, as well as flourishing theories, and selected the ones I believe best describe the changes we go through after the age of 30. Our knowledge of the natural differences that occur at various ages can help us understand why we feel the way we feel after 30 and perhaps allow us to accept where we are at, rather than beat ourselves up for feeling less happy.

What makes it challenging to assess happiness changes after 30 is not only the various theories of well-being, but also the traditional outlook on happiness, which is lack of ill-being. Let us look at this concept a little closer.

The battle of ill-being and well-being

Frank contacted me after three years of intense therapy. When I met him, he no longer suffered from depression, and had managed to successfully wean himself off antidepressants. However, despite getting the all-clear from his GP, he did not feel happy. *How is it possible?* – he wondered – *It is like I can see it is out there, yet it continues to be out of my reach.* Even though he was very confused, what he said made a lot of sense to me.

For many years when psychologists measured ill-being, they assumed that as long as we do not have depression, anxiety, or any other pathologies, we are ok[28]. Therefore, as soon as their patients ceased to report their symptoms of ill-being, they were, just like my client, classified as healthy. This is a very one-dimensional view of well-being, which is considerably more complex. Here is how psychologists discovered its intricacies.

A few years ago, data from thousands of people aged 25 to 74 years was reviewed and participants were divided into groups[29]. The first group included everyone with symptoms of mental illness, such as major depression, anxiety, panic disorder, or alcohol dependence. The second group included those who were doing psychologically well, whilst the final group were people who flourished in life.

Curiously, as the researcher continued to analyse data, another group began to emerge: languishers. They were the 12.1% of people who were neither happy nor sad, just like Frank. Even though they did not have any mental illness, neither did they have mental health. The odd thing was that when contrasted with those who reported mental illness, languishers were less engaged with life, less aware as to what they wanted out of life, less likely to set goals, or take actions to change their situation for the better. In other words, these individuals were traditionally diagnosed as not suffering from mental illness, however, their psychological state was not good, and in some ways, even worse than those who were diagnosed with mental illness.

Sometimes, when we are faced with the prospect of mental illness, in other words, when we believe we have hit rock bottom, it motivates us to make a change in our lives. It gives us the courage to finally ask for help and allows us to make sense of what is happening to us. This may be why those who are already experiencing symptoms of depression may engage with life more than people who are languishing, and set goals to get themselves out of their tricky situation. Moreover, despite being considered free from mental illness, languishers were at a very high risk of experiencing it over the next 12 months. Compared to those who were well, their likelihood of being sick was doubled; and in comparison to the flourishing individuals, they were six times more likely to have a mental illness in the near future. Yet, these people were previously viewed as doing psychologically well, and no effort was made to prevent an onset of their mental illness.

This study made us realise that there is more to wellness than the absence of illness. The evidence for viewing wellness in this manner came from two researchers based at the University of Cambridge. They carried out studies with people who were diagnosed with depression, and found that 35.1% of those with mental health issues such as depression, anxiety, and alcoholism, also experienced some components of well-being[30]. Thus, just because we have mental health issues, does not mean we cannot also experience symptoms of wellness, such as meaning in life, or sense of achievement.

Symptoms of well-being help us cope with ill-being more effectively. For instance, when we experience a higher level of positive emotions before undergoing a highly stressful situation, we bounce back from this adversity faster, and feel better sooner[31]. Therefore, positive emotions add this special something to improve our well-being.

That said, ill-being and well-being work in tandem. Experiencing depression may still affect our happiness, as curiously, there is an inverted U-shaped depression, which follows a similar age pattern as

U-shaped happiness. Thus, we experience the highest levels of depression around the late 30s and early 40s[32], whereas our probability of using antidepressants is at its highest at around the age of 45[33], which means it lags after the depression diagnosis. This is why, in the current book, I did not just focus on components of well-being, but also reviewed the literature relating to ill-being. After all, if ill-being makes us less happy, we need to know what drives these changes after 30.

The journey

This book will take you on a journey of what I believe are five main reasons for changes in our well-being after 30. They are: the perception of time and its effect on our minds and behaviours; our experiences of positive emotions, which alter as we age; the changes in our social networks throughout our lifespan, which have a significant impact on our happiness; the experiences of life adversities, which fluctuate throughout our lifespan; and an ability to make sense of our lives and predict behaviours.

These reasons are not exhaustive, as literature suggests several other changes that may explain the U-shaped happiness. However, this book offers a starting point for discussing such changes. It serves as a platform for a different way of viewing happiness, which is a natural process that alters throughout our lifespan, rather than a destination.

As we journey through our lives, we continually learn new life skills, which allow us to tackle our challenges more effectively, as well as help us feel happier and appreciate what we have in our lives that little bit more. We change as people over the course of our lives. We constantly evolve. It is an active process that allows us to make mistakes, suffer the temporary consequences, learn from them, and potentially thrive thereafter. Let us embrace the changes and trust our journey. It might take us to some wonderful places that are worth going to, even though the road might not always be as smooth as we like it.

After reading this book, you might still want to take action to change your well-being, be it by practicing some Positive Psychology activities, such as mindfulness, or engaging in physical exercise, simply because you have read that they can boost your well-being. Taking action to enhance our lives is a good thing, as long as we do not beat ourselves up if it doesn't work for us as well as we had expected. If that happens, let us not put ourselves under unnecessary pressure. Life will teach us ways to handle challenges more effectively in the future.

Our natural changes associated with aging, as well as the skills we learn on our way, may allow us to live a better life in years to come. All we need to do is be conscious of where we are at.

Our knowledge of this active process will help us become more engaged passengers on the life-journey. We will have acute awareness of what is happening to us today, and will be able to predict better and perhaps change our future. Most importantly, however, it will offer us the hope that, no matter what stage we are at, our lives can always get even better.

TIME-TRAVELS

I can still remember the day I learnt that I could time-travel. In a matter of a split-second I was able to revisit the good old times, or transport myself all the way into the bright future. I did not need to lose myself in a science fiction book or movie, nor did I require any complicated equipment to help me on my way. All I needed was just me and my mind, and it all began with Zimbardo.

A few decades ago, when one of the most famous psychologists, Philip Zimbardo, was attending secondary school, he realised that despite speaking English, people around him seemed to be communicating differently. He came from an Italian-American family that instilled in him living in the moment values. They would meet in the evening, eat, laugh, and have fun. Their life philosophy was to enjoy the here and now without any worry about tomorrow.

At the same time, when he went to school, his teachers did not use the same language to describe life. They did not talk about fun, or laughter, or the here and now, rather about studying for a test in two weeks, preparing for exams in two years, and considering a job he might want to do in 20 years. Despite both speaking English, his family and school communicated differently; they lived in different time perspectives.

School teaches us the importance of focusing on the future. This is a particularly difficult task for students, because as children we are naturally prone to enjoy the present[34]. We play, have fun, and lose ourselves in our daily activities, only to be yanked back by the teachers reminding us that we have to study today for better results tomorrow. This is why adolescents who are able to dip into the future for longer, and allow the future to guide their present behaviour, have higher academic achievement[35], are less likely to get into trouble in school[36], and are ultimately more successful in life[37]. They are able to see the consequences of their actions, which allows them to make wiser choices.

This is not surprising. After all, a wise man once said that if you gave him six hours to chop down a tree, he would spend the first four sharpening his axe. This is a great example of future thinking. It allowed him to project himself into the future, see what he needed to do in the present to prepare for it, and then take action to make it happen. If instead of planning ahead, he focused his attention on having fun for the first few hours, chances are he would not be very successful at completing his task. This is why students who are focused on the future are better prepared, which results in them achieving higher grade averages than those focused on enjoying the present [38]. At the same time, however, predominantly future-oriented people are ultimately less happy as they miss out on having fun and living a care-free life [39].

As we enter our 20s, our future thinking becomes even more prominent than it was before. We imagine our new life, perfect family, comfortable home, and ideal job; and those images help us make it all happen. During our 20s, we see our future as this vast field of possibilities. Such focus helps us shape our lives and allows us to become the best versions of ourselves.

Those of us who are particularly good at focusing on the future invest time and effort to prepare for it. Thus, our future focus is somewhat good for us, as it makes us ultimately healthier both physically and mentally. At the same time, future-focus is also associated with ambiguity [40], which is why it can make us feel more anxious as we journey through our 20s and 30s.

Meet Sharon, one of my friends, who is now a 40-something happily married woman with two teenage kids. She met her husband in college, where they hung out with each other enjoying the good old Irish craic. When she was in her mid-20s, she embarked on a fabulous career, which saw her promoted from one position to another, finally allowing her to become a senior manager in a medium sized company. Once her new career began to grow, her then boyfriend asked her to marry him. They had a wonderful wedding, bought a beautiful house, had two gorgeous kids and in the midst of it all, a lot of uncertainty about their future.

When she reflects upon her 20s and 30s, she always describes them as a maze of life. Despite her life going reasonably well, or at least the way she was hoping it would go, she remembers her 20s and 30s as swimming through uncharted territories. She had to experience the *first* job, the *first* project, the *first* date, the *first* meeting of the future in-laws, the *first* day after getting married, the *first* period after they tried to get pregnant and did not succeed, the *first* sickness of their child. In other words, the *first* of everything, and constant dilemmas, as to what decision to make and how it will all turn out. All these ongoing changes in her life, as well as building it up into what she wanted it to be, were associated with uncertainty. This created ambiguity in relation to her future, which made her less happy.

As she grew older, there were still the *first* things happening to her, however, they were significantly easier to cope with after all the other decisions she had made to bring her to this point. Today, in her late 40s, unless a huge adversity occurs, she can predict her future life a little bit better and there seems to be less ambiguity to deal with every day. The *foundations* of her life, i.e. her husband, kids, friends, and job, are all in place. The *cosmetics* of her life might change, but overall she is clear enough as to where it is all heading. With less ambiguity, she experiences more peace of mind, thus feels a little happier about her lot. This may be one of the reasons as to why our happiness grows as we pass the turbulent mid 30s and 40s.

Shrinking future

As we grow older, our time perspective changes. We realise that our future shrinks every day, therefore, we want to grab the bull by the horns and find ways to enjoy what we have left. This positivity focus becomes a prominent part of our lives, and we will discuss it in more detail in the next chapter. However, as our future shrinks, we also want to avoid as much negativity in our lives as we can. One way of doing so is by cultivating forgiveness. Research shows that as we age, we are more likely to forgive others [41], because we realise that life becomes too short to hold grudges.

The nature of forgiveness is often misunderstood by people who see it as a justification of wrongdoings, condoning someone's behaviour, or even worse, excusing their behaviour due to extenuating circumstances that made them act in this manner. However, from the psychological perspective, there is more to forgiveness than this.

One of my clients, Carole, was dating a man who she began slowly to fall in love with. They lived miles apart from each other, however, despite the distance, he made sure to see her regularly. Every other weekend, and sometimes more often, he would drive all the way to her place, shower her with presents, treat her like a princess, and attend to her every need. He was almost too good to be true. After her friends met him for the first time, they all said he was a keeper, and she felt grateful for having him in her life.

One day, three months after their first date, one of her girlfriends walked down a street, when suddenly she turned, and without thinking twice, waved her hand at a jeep passing by and yelled: *Hey Tony!* She saw Carole's boyfriend behind the steering wheel. As soon as she yelled, her eyes fell on a woman sitting next to him. It was not Carole. And then she saw two kids in the back. *Hold on* – she thought – *maybe it is not Tony.* She looked closer at the man driving the jeep and she knew it was definitely him. Then, the woman sitting next to him looked at her frowning, turned to Tony and he drove away, as if nothing happened. This odd encounter left Carole confused, and she tried to contact him to clarify the situation. His phone number, however, was soon disconnected, leaving her with more questions than answers. After a three-month whirl-wind romance she never saw or spoke with Tony again.

This experience made her feel stupid, and betrayed (her own words). She could not understand why he had lied to her for over three months, and felt annoyed with herself for not realising that he had lived a double life. There were so many signs; small inconsistencies she chose to ignore, because she wanted to trust him completely. The thoughts about his wrongdoings made her upset and she kept replaying them in her mind: *How could he have done it? What a monster he was to me, and even worse, to his family! How did I not see it? What is wrong with me for not seeing this?*

It took Carole ages to forgive him. In the end, she knew it was the best thing for her to do. Not forgiving meant that she allowed him to cheat on her over and over again in her head. Going through all these painful thoughts, a few times a day, was just too much to bear. Forgiveness was the only option.

Forgiveness is not about making the perpetrator feel good. Instead, it is about the person who suffered the wrongdoing letting go of all negative emotions associated with the event as well as the perpetrator, and allowing peace into their heart and mind. Once we manage to replace negativity with positivity, it boosts our *psychological well-being*[42] and helps us feel better. When we forgive, our bodies also change, as they begin to experience less stress, our heart rate and blood pressure decrease, and we feel calmer[43]. Since our bodies affect our minds, forgiveness brings more peace into our lives.

It takes time and effort to forgive. Forgiveness is not an easy process, but the good news is that as we age, we are more likely to forgive others for their wrongdoings[44]. It may be because we are more aware of our future shrinking, so we prefer to spend as much time as we can feeling good. Holding grudges causes us to experience symptoms of anxiety and anger, which make our lives less enjoyable. Life is too short for this, which is why we choose to forgive more as we grow older.

Our capacity to forgive others later on in life, may be another reason as to why life becomes happier after the initial dip in midlife. This is a worthwhile lesson to learn. Perhaps, if we manage to bring forgiveness into our lives sooner, it would save us a lot of hardship on the way. Seeing our future as shrinking may give us that kick-start to let go of grudges and live a happier life.

Balancing it all out

The wonderful thing about time perspectives is that at any given time, we can move along the time spectrum. Sometimes it happens automatically, other times we can consciously make it happen. Therefore, in a matter of a split second our thoughts can take us into the past, help us stay in the present, or move us into the future.

We can recall what we were up to yesterday, try and catch our scarf that has just blown away in the wind, or think of what we are planning to do tomorrow. Each one of these thoughts can be positive or negative. Therefore, the events we recall from yesterday may be happy or painful, we can choose to catch the scarf or decide there is no point in trying to do so as the wind is too strong, or we can think of tomorrow with optimism or dread.

Each of these perspectives will evoke different emotions in us and result in various consequences. For example, spending a lot of time thinking about the positive past will make us feel happy and grounded. Thinking about the negative past may result in us feeling sad or angry. Trying to catch the scarf can make us laugh a lot as we struggle with the wind, or elicit helplessness if we choose not to do anything about it. Also, future time perspective boosts either feelings of anxiety or hopefulness depending on how we view it. Therefore, each of these perspectives comes with consequences.

Researchers found that sometimes, just like Marty McFly from *Back to the Future,* we get stuck in one time perspective, which means that it is harder for us to move along the time spectrum[45]. On the other hand, when we have a balanced time perspective, we can freely move from one perspective to another as we need to[46].

For example, many gamblers are stuck in the present time perspective[47]. They go to a casino, begin to play, and all they think about is the here and now. They do not consider the fact that if they spend all their money today, they will not have enough to pay their mortgage tomorrow. On the other hand, when someone can flexibly move along the spectrum, they will know when to enjoy a spot of gambling and will stop as soon as they see they spent all the money they planned to spend on it.

Our balanced time perspective consists of spending significant time thinking of the positive past and enjoying ourselves in the present, with a little bit less time spent thinking about the future, and even less time focusing on a negative past and present sense of giving up. As we age, however, our time perspectives may shift towards the past.

Good old times

A few years ago I took my mum and her sister for a girly summer weekend away. We went to Cracow, a medieval city in Poland bursting with history and culture. We walked down a cobbled street laughing away at every opportunity when my mum spotted a beautiful café near the market square and suggested we stop there for lunch. As we walked through an archway into a walled garden, we saw it covered with plants dancing to a gentle summer breeze and could hear the birds singing so loud that human sounds disappeared into the background. It was magical.

The waitress approached us dressed up in a medieval costume and gave us a warm and honest smile as she guided us to a table resting in the shade of a tree. After we ordered our food, I excused myself from the table to go to the ladies and when I came back I knew that something was seriously off.

I could see it from a distance as I approached the table. My aunt was highly animated, her face flushed, her voice raised. She was telling my mum a story about this woman who yelled at her, then took a ruler and slapped the top of her hand so hard it burnt. As I watched my aunt quivering, I became worried about her weak heart. *Auntie, are you ok? Who slapped you?* – I urged, wondering what happened in the last five minutes that made my relaxed auntie so highly emotional – *I told you!* – she rebuked – Miss Kowalska. – *Who is Miss Kowalska?* – I asked confused as my aunt looked at me surprised – *My history teacher.*

The beautiful medieval surroundings of the café made my aunt think of history, which, in turn brought up lots of memories about her history teacher who was mean to her over 50 years ago. From a psychological viewpoint, my aunt is a great example of someone who lives in a predominantly past time perspective. Daily cues bring her back very quickly into the past, significantly affecting her present state of mind. That day it was negative, but some days all she talks about are positive past events.

Research shows us that when we recall a lot of negative past events and believe that we cannot really influence our lives, we are less likely to feel content with our lot[48]. On the other hand, happier people spend more time thinking about positive past experiences, a little less amount of time enjoying the present moment, and even less amount of time hoping for a happier future[49]. Therefore, living regularly through positive past experiences is a crucial ingredient for feeling happier, as it allows us to consider where we came from and feel proud and capable to make more such memories in the future. We can still recall some bad times, every now and then, and learn from our negative experiences. However, our focus is mainly on the positive rather than negative. In other words, our time perspective is more balanced.

The good news is that as we age, and our future shrinks, we usually turn to the past to help us fill up our thoughts[50]. This is a coping mechanism we develop to allow us to make sense of the time passing by. Besides, in the autumn and winter of our lives we carry a lot of memories from our past, and are more likely to recall them doing what we do every day. Let me give you an example.

As I mentioned earlier, I live in Dublin, a small city on the east coast of Ireland, which for me, is filled with memories. Yesterday, we were visiting our friends who have just bought a house. As we were driving into their estate, I was commenting to my husband on the places we passed by. One of the houses on my friends' road reminded me of a house around my local area, which is absolutely covered with coming Christmas decorations during the festive season. That made me remember my past Christmases and think how excited I am about this Christmas. Then, as we turned into my friends' cul-de-sac, I commented on how well their neighbours looked after their homes. This reminded me of the first house we bought and the types of neighbours we have had over the years. I went on a journey of recalling the good old memories.

This is what happens to us as we age. Over the years we gather a lot of memories. They are ready for us to bring to the surface and it is as if we seek out opportunities to do so. We become skilled at recalling them with a simple cue. This helps to take our attention away from our ultimate destination. If we did not do it, we might become paralysed with the anxiety associated with death. Focusing on the past helps us to adjust better.

Apart from the anxiety, our past focus when we age allows us to fulfil our generativity needs[51]. By this, I mean that we feel like our time on this earth was worthwhile and we have done something that contributes to future generations. This is why, we freely recall our past lessons and share them with younger people.

Our thinking about the past, specifically what we have done and how we have arrived at this point in time, allows us also to feel more confident and comfortable in ourselves. They are all attributes of a healthy mind; thus, reflecting upon the past may contribute to us feeling happier.

What helps us feel well is our positive past-focus. Research shows that as we age, we are more likely to recall positive, rather than negative past events [52]. Of course, we may have some regrets, lessons learnt, and we may even feel hard done by someone in the past. However, it is the positive, not negative memories that are flowing effortlessly into our minds, enhancing our experiences of positive emotions and making our lives that little bit happier.

I remember being surprised when I witnessed my nanna's positive focus while lying on her deathbed. As she held my hand she was telling me about the wonderful and blessed life she had. In that moment, she did not recall the atrocities of WW2, challenges she experienced during her midlife with her six children, or the death of my grandfather, who she desperately missed. Instead, all she could think about were all the good things that had happened to her. She was able to recall her children and grandchildren being born, the places she saw, the wonderful things she did. All negativity faded away, as she bathed in her positive memories from the past. She died in her 80s and was the happiest I had ever seen her.

We are created to survive, which is why we learn and adjust as we age. When our future seems limitless, we think about it a lot. We plan what we will do, and the type of people we want to become. Whilst this blank canvas may inspire us, it can also cause ambiguity, which is one of the reasons why we might feel less happy in our midlife.

Later on, however, as our future shrinks we spend more time recalling our past. This is our coping mechanism that helps us come to terms with the inevitable end. Thinking too much about the future might leave us scared and anxious. On the other hand, this past-focus helps us experience more positivity, develop confidence, and makes us feel like we have contributed positively to the world. Here again, our clever psyche helps us focus our attention on the good stuff, leaving the negatives behind. Since what we focus on becomes our reality, all these changes may also be a reason why we feel happier as we age.

HEART AND MIND

A few years ago, I was taken into a cold room, sat on a hard chair, and forced to watch a clip that was meant to upset me. It featured all that could potentially go wrong in my life, and which I usually do not want to think too much about. My experience was a little disturbing, but I was willing to do it in the name of science. That day I participated in a psychological experiment, the objective of which was to discover the benefits of positive emotions. Yes, positive, not negative emotions.

Whilst I, and 34 other people in the room tried to desperately turn our heads away from the upsetting images, and cover our ears to reduce the effect of the gloomy music, the other group of 35 randomly selected people enjoyed a three-minute clip showing them all the best that life can offer. They saw adorable babies, pictures of joy and laughter, marriage, love, graduation, family and friends, in other words the height of happiness.

After both groups watched their clips, researchers asked us to solve a problem, specifically, to come up with as many creative ways to use a paper clip as we could. Considering our state of mind, we were proud to have come up with 34 ideas. At the same time, the *happy* group were able to think of 74 solutions to their problem. When they debriefed us, we could not believe it! We were all psychologists, smart, generally healthy, yet our creativity was severely diminished by our negative emotions.

For many years, psychologists believed that positive emotions are simply opposites of negative emotions and do not deserve much time and effort to be studied as separate entities[53]. Negative emotions, on the other hand, got a lot of good press, for serving a great, evolutionary purpose, of helping us survive. They act as a warning sign telling us that we need to make some changes in our lives. When we feel sad, it could mean that we have something very important missing in our lives, for example the hope of a happy future with our former partner, before we decided to break up. This realisation could motivate us to summon all the energy we have left, go out there and meet new people in an attempt to hopefully change our circumstances. When we feel angry, it could mean that our values are being questioned, or someone took something from us that we worked very hard to get, so we need to stand up for ourselves and fight the injustice of it. Therefore, the purpose of negative emotions is to help us get our lives back on track and reach our ultimate goal to survive.

On the other hand, positive emotions did not appear to serve any high-level purpose. Every time I asked people what, in their opinion, was the purpose of positive emotions, they would simply say: to make us happy. Anything else? – I would probe further, and it is at this point that I was usually hit by a wall of silence. Yet, recent research shows us they serve a whole array of very important purposes, which we can draw from as we age.

What's so good about positivity?

In the nineties, a psychologist from the University of North Carolina, Barbara Fredrickson, became interested in positive emotions and their benefits to humankind. Having read all the research relating to positive emotions, she found that broadly speaking, there are three ways in which they can serve us.

Firstly, they allow us to see a broader perspective on things. Thus, just as the experiment I participated in, we are able to see more solutions to our problems when experiencing positive emotions. We are more creative and see more options, which help us expand our knowledge and skills. When experiencing positivity, our world opens up, allowing additional information to flow in; information that is typically not available to us when experiencing negative emotions.

Negativity, on the other hand, makes us more rigid, constricted, and narrows our minds so that we can see less options to choose from. This narrow mindset is there for a reason, it helps us preserve our energy to fight danger, or make a change, rather than frivolously spending it on making choices from a wide pool of options. Let me offer you an example of it.

A few years ago, I was stopped at the traffic lights at a busy junction in Dublin. It was raining heavily, but I like the rain, so did not mind the difficult conditions. When the lights turned green, everybody moved on. We drove 30km/hour when suddenly the jeep in front of me slammed on his breaks. As soon as he did it, all my positive emotions and thoughts of what I was planning to do over the weekend disappeared and were replaced with fear. As I slammed on my breaks, my car started to aquaplane. I lost control over my breaks and all I could think of were two choices I had: 1. *Will I hit the jeep in front of me head on?* or 2. *Will I turn the car into the ditch and roll?* When in danger, my mind narrowed down my choices, so that I would not have to spend too much energy thinking about them. I could have been thinking about getting out of the car, or covering my face, or turning into the opposite direction from the ditch, but it would not be useful for me, as I was about to crash my car, so I could only recall thinking of these two choices. This is how negative emotions narrowed my mind, to help me survive.

Positive emotions, on the other hand, open up our repertoire of actions. Once I got out of the car after the crash, the driver in front of me ran over to see if I was ok. Whilst my car looked like a write-off, there was hardly a scratch on his jeep. As we waited for the towing truck to arrive, we sat on the side of the road joking about the absurdity of it all. Soon, I began to see opportunities I have had to avoid the accident. They were not available to me during the crash, because at that point it was too late to call upon them. This is what positive emotions do for us, open up our minds to find better solutions to our challenges.

Another benefit of positive emotions is that they help us recover after experiencing negative emotions. For example, when after the crash, the other driver and I sat on the side of the road chatting this simple act made me smile, feel better about the situation and helped us both recover from the shock of a crash.

Something similar happened to us after participating in the psychological experiment. Those in the negative group were shaken up by the images we saw, which is why the researchers made us listen to Louis Armstrong's song, *What a Wonderful World* three times, so that we would spend nine minutes bathing in the lyrics and melody of happiness and hopefulness, in order to balance out the three minutes of sadness and despair. They had to do it, because negativity is more powerful and lasts longer than positivity, and so it takes more time to bring us back to the emotionally neutral place.

There are consequences of leaving ourselves in a negative place for too long. In a US study, when participants' emotions were not brought back to neutral or positive, they experienced heighted levels of worry, and ruminative thoughts (these are thoughts that keep nagging us over and over again), even 24 hours later[54]. This is why an ability to manage our emotions in a way that brings out positivity is like sitting on a gold mine. It makes our life experiences richer, more positive, and ultimately happier.

Furthermore, experiencing positive emotions serves as a resource-builder. When we experience, on average, more positive than negative emotions, we build psychological, social, physical and intellectual resources that help us cope better with life adversities. They act like a shield protecting us from the negative force.

In a study carried out before and after 9/11, the researchers found that those who had a wider repertoire of positive emotions prior to the 9/11 adversity, were more resilient and able to bounce back faster after the event. When we have a resource of positive emotions that we can draw from, we are more likely to find meaning in difficult situations[55], as well as find it easier to cope with adversity. Having easy access to positive emotions allows us to draw from them at any stage when we need them.

These are all reasons as to why positive emotions are a crucial foundation for happiness. Without them, we would find it more difficult to feel good, content, or fulfilled in life. Thus, an ability to manage our positive emotions, and draw from their resource is invaluable. Curiously, as we age, this is exactly what we become proficient at doing.

Emotional stability

I met Carina whilst working in a call centre, my first grown-up job. We were employed there through a recruitment agency that, as we found out later, frequently collaborated with our organisation. Both Carina and I were interviewed by Martin, an Irish guy in his late 20s, who was also invited to our staff party.

It was organised on the roof terrace of our company building. There was a band playing in the background, caterers walking around with platters full of tasty BBQ food and a lot of people swaying around to the sound of music and enjoying glasses of vino, which was poured freely throughout the evening. In other words, the party was like any other staff party we have all been to, except this one has remained in my memory forever. Half way through the event, I heard a commotion. When I turned around to check what was happening, I saw Martin, surrounded by a group of girls, and Carina walking away nonchalantly from the crowd, with a big smile on her face.

Later on, I found out that after Martin interviewed her for a job, he asked her out and they began dating. As soon as they became intimate, he started screening her calls, and subsequently, they never met again. That is, until the day, when she saw him on the roof terrace surrounded by other girls, flirting their heads off. She felt both betrayed and humiliated, which is why, she grabbed a glass of red wine, marched towards him, and threw it onto his face making the whole group of women jump. When describing it later, she said she had felt like she had no control over her emotions. It was, as if something inside her made her pick up the glass and throw the wine at him.

I lost touch with Carina, until one day, a few years ago, when I bumped into her on the street. We were delighted to see each other, so we went to the local café and sat there for hours catching up with our lives and recalling the good old times. That's when I mentioned what happened at the party. *Gosh* – Carina reflected in response – *I used to be so hot-headed. Nowadays, I do not even get annoyed. I think to myself: what's the point in getting myself all worked up? It won't solve anything and will only waste my energy.*

I was not surprised when I heard Carina say that she is no longer controlled by her emotions. As we age, we are less likely to over-react to situations[56]. When faced with an adversity, we are less likely to consider it threatening to us[57], instead we tend to believe that we have adequate skills to cope with it more effectively.

A significant advantage of aging is that our emotions become more stable[58]. When younger adults (aged 20-30) were compared with older people (aged 70-80), they showed a significant fluctuation of both positive and negative emotions. These constant changes of our emotional states can be tiring. I remember my parents in their late 30s and 40s; small things would spark them off each other. One minute they were fine, next minute they were arguing about something. I remember thinking at the time how unpredictable they were. As they aged, however, it is as if they became different people. They were more placid and balanced in the way they lived their lives. The last few years before my dad passed away, my parents really enjoyed each other's company and rarely ever argued. They lived an emotionally stable life, which is what happens to many of us as we age.

Choosing positivity

How much of your day do you spend experiencing positive and negative emotions? If you are not sure how to answer this, try and become more aware of your emotions over the next few days. Watch out for how they change. Catch yourself at various moments and try to name how you feel, to help you make sense of what is going on inside you. This is a very powerful exercise. You may be surprised with the diversity of your daily emotional experiences. Alternatively, if you are anything like me, you might turn to a psychological questionnaire[59], which will show you not only what type of emotions you experience daily, i.e. positive or negative, but also their ratio.

Researchers found that people who flourish in life appear to have a significantly higher ratio of positive to negative emotions[60]. Specifically, it was suggested that they experience at least three positive emotions to one negative emotion. To simplify it, imagine you have an argument with your spouse. During this short outburst, you may experience anger. According to this research, in order to neutralise its effect, you need to engage in activities that fill you up with at least three experiences of hopefulness, awe, or joy. Negativity is way more powerful than positivity, thus we require more positive emotions to balance out negatives.

Whilst the premise of the 3:1 positivity ratio has been questioned by other researchers[61] and subsequently withdrawn[62], the notion of experiencing more positive than negative emotions remains[63]. Thus, feelings of higher levels of positivity continue to be a significant predictor of a good life.

The question, however, is whether our experiences of the positivity ratio change throughout our lifespan. Consider yourself now and 10 years ago. Have your positive emotions increased or decreased in the last decade? Research shows that those below the age of 39 reported the lowest levels of positive compared to negative emotions[64]. It appears that as we move into our 40s and 50s, through to very old age our ratio becomes more positive.

Furthermore, other studies indicated similar results. They showed that the experiences of positive emotions decrease in our late 30s, and then systematically increase after the age of 40[65]. This means that as we grow older, we are more likely to experience emotions such as joy, gratitude, love, serenity, hope, interest, pride, amusement, inspiration, awe, and many others. They become a more consistent part of our lives, which may be the cause for U-shaped happiness.

In a way, it makes sense. Year by year, as we tackle challenges, we learn how to manoeuvre through life with more finesse. I remember that when I was in my 20s, I was delivering a training event for a group of 40 people when suddenly, half-way through my presentation, the overhead projector broke down. Flooded with a fear of failure and good old-fashioned panic, I cut the session short and retrieved into my cave for a few hours trying to pick up my confidence.

Last week, almost 20 years later, I experienced a similar situation. I was invited to address an audience at an international event. When I arrived,

I found out that their audio-visual equipment failed, so I had to stand up in front of hundreds of people and deliver my presentation without any slideshow. I was nervous, but I did it. Quite frankly, I really loved the challenge of doing it so differently. This was possibly one of my best talks, which subsequently filled me up with pride, a sense of achievement, and satisfaction. My past life experiences helped me become more confident when dealing with this tricky situation. This may be one of the reasons why we become happier as we grow older.

Emotional complexity

When I was a child, I loved playgrounds, especially the one near where my granny lived. It belonged to a kindergarten and was only used by children attending it with the strict supervision of their teachers. However, since I was quite a rebellious child, over the weekend, when the kindergarten was closed, my friends and I used to jump over the fence and play there for hours.

What I loved about this playground was that it was in good nick, very colourful, and absolutely enormous. It was built over an acre of land and had many things to keep us occupied. My favourite was a seesaw. It was the biggest I have ever seen. When one of us was at the bottom, the other one went up so high that we could look into first floor apartments. I loved it!

Today, when I think of seesaws, our emotional lives spring to my mind. For many years, psychologists believed that our emotions are like a seesaw; they keep changing from positive to negative throughout the day. We hug our loved ones, and experience a burst of happiness; we get bad news, our emotions change immediately to negative. Therefore, we go between the extremes of positive and negative emotions like children going up and down on a seesaw.

However, whilst this may be true for some, other people's emotions are more complex, whereby they experience a mixture of positive and negative emotions all at the same time[66]. Here is a simple example of how it may work. I met my husband when we were both in our 20s, living our lives to the full and riding a seesaw of emotions every day. Just like many other young people, we moved constantly between positive and negative emotions, our world at the time was more black and white.

One day, as we sat on a beanbag (which was very cool at the time!), in the comfort of our new home, we saw an enormous spider walking across the floor.

Petrified of spiders, I screamed, Brendan jumped, and flooded with lots of negative emotions, he instantly launched at and killed the intruder.

Roll on 20 years, and now in our early to mid-40s, we are having a friend over for dinner. The three of us are sitting at the table, talking about something, laughing away, when my friend spots a spider, points at it, shudders and goes: *Oh God, look at it. I hate spiders.* We all turn our heads in the spider's direction. Brendan, still not enjoying having them in the house, stands up, picks it up gently and throws it outside onto the grass. His reaction nowadays is not as extreme as it used to be, because today, apart from the fear, he is also aware of experiencing other emotions, such as love and empathy for all living creatures. This is why, instead of automatically killing the spider, his emotional complexity allowed him make a choice of saving its life by removing it from our sight.

This type of emotional development is not unusual. Research shows that as we grow older, our emotions become significantly more complex, allowing us to experience positive and negative emotions at the same time [67]. Mind you, many people have this awareness regardless of their age. However, as we grow older, we become even more proficient at managing the complexities of our emotional reactions. This is a helpful strategy for dealing with such situations as losses in our lives.

My dad passed away well over a decade ago. I often have a big smile on my face when I think about him. I remember our last dinner together, all the banter over the years, and my admiration with how quickly he was able to solve a crossword puzzle. He had such an amazingly sharp mind, up until the very last moment. All these wonderful memories allow me to experience a burst of positive emotions, whilst at the same time, I am also feeling a pang of sadness that he is gone, and I long to have one last conversation with him. These bitter-sweet moments are part of life and a healthy sign of our adaptation [68]. They help us regulate our losses in life, such as people that are no longer here, just like my dad, or experiencing our body and mind declining as we grow older [69]. Despite all the negative changes that occur as we age, we seem to feel more and more fulfilled, and ultimately happier, as we enter the autumn and winter of our lives.

Emotional coping

With time, we also learn more effective techniques on how to cope with daily life situations. Midlife is full of daily hassles, ranging from running errands, to balancing work and personal life. We support people around us, yet sometimes find it challenging to look after ourselves. When life challenges get on top of us, we either go into denial and pretend they do not exist, or try and resolve our problems, by improving our mood, or taking control of the situations or our reactions to them.

Inability to flex our style in the face of daily challenges, and sweeping the problems under the carpet, may result in us experiencing mood disorders. Some of us are lucky to have learnt effective coping techniques from our parents or other people around us, when we were younger. Others learn them later on in their lives.

In a famous longitudinal study that followed people for over seven decades[70], the researchers found that even those from less privileged backgrounds, who did not learn effective coping skills in early life, may have lost their way in their 20s or 30s but then recovered. Often times, they met people on their life journey who helped them learn the ropes. These people were usually their spouses, friends, and sometimes even work colleagues. Learning from them resulted in increases of well-being later on in life. Therefore, with age comes life experiences that allow us to develop our coping skills.

Research is largely consistent in relation to this. As we continue to age, our coping strategies change. When we experience life challenges in our midlife, we tend to cope by confronting others, seeking out social support, and planning how to solve our problems[71]. On the other hand, as we grow older, our coping mechanisms become more passive, as we learn to distance ourselves from unnecessary negativity, accept our responsibilities, and look on the bright side of the situations we find ourselves in. All these changes that occur after 40 allow us to live a more positive and rewarding life.

As we age, we learn about ourselves and others. Our feelings become more complex, thus allowing us to experience both sadness and happiness at the same time. This complexity not only makes more sense to us, but it also feels comfortable, thus allowing us to feel ok in this grey territory of emotions. With this comes more stability, thus we are no longer on a seesaw of emotions, rather we regulate our feelings so that we stay in a calmer, less intense place.

As our emotional intelligence grows, we become more familiar with the consequences of negativity, therefore, choose to focus on positivity and develop skills to sustain our positive emotions for longer. Add to it an improved ability to cope with our emotions and all these emotional changes become one of the most important reasons as to why we are happier as we age.

PADDING FOR LIFE

I have always wondered what it felt like to have depression. I used to work for Samaritans, a helpline devoted to helping people who suffered from it, sometimes to such an extent that they considered taking their own lives. As I listened to the callers and asked them questions, I tried to imagine what it was like to be in their shoes. My curiosity was soon satisfied, as following the death of my grandmother, then my father, and a few other disastrous events in my life that occurred soon after, I was diagnosed with depression.

Depression often creeps in so slowly that before we notice, it has become very hard to cope with. The symptoms of depression are like bear cubs moving onto an island that only we inhabit. As they come onto the island one by one, we do not feel too threatened by them, because we believe we can easily manage them. After all, they are small and harmless. However, over time they grow into full size grizzly bears and it becomes impossible to share with them our small island, whilst at the same time continuing to feel safe.

The same applies to depression. The symptoms can come on slowly and it may take us a long time before we realise we have it. Symptoms may include difficulties associated with sleep, i.e. sleeping too much, not enough, or waking up frequently throughout the night; experiencing prolonged bouts of negative feelings, such as sadness, anxiety, or anger; having low energy; losing interest in hobbies and in spending time with family and friends; poor concentration or slowed-down thinking; and suicidal thoughts. Once we experience five symptoms or more, lasting a fortnight or longer, our GP or mental health professional may diagnose us with depression.

For some, diagnosis may come as a relief, as they have known for a while that something was not ok, but could not figure out what exactly was the problem. For others, being diagnosed becomes a burden, as it is yet another problem they need to solve. Such a diagnosis is particularly tricky for mental health professionals, such as myself, who are there to help others, yet are going through their own challenging times.

My depression lasted a total of 13 months, and I remember thinking that I could not wait to recover from it. My curiosity about it was satisfied and I did not like feeling that way. Also, being a mental health professional, I knew that it was temporary, and I just needed to find the strength in me to cope with all the losses in my life, accept them, and move on. In the meantime, I did not want people around me to see me that way, so at work I put on a brave face, whilst at home I withdrew from my circle of friends and excused myself every time they tried to connect with me.

Withdrawing from others made my situation worse. I felt more lonely and distant from the people that could have potentially helped me. I buried my head in the sand hoping the storm would pass, and it was only when I hit rock bottom that I finally reached out to my friends and family. I rang them one by one and asked if they wanted to meet. They did, and meeting up with them again marked the beginning of my journey to recovery.

Today, I am grateful for this ordeal and a year of sadness, as it made me realise the importance of people in my life. Nowadays, whenever my life goes off track a little, I make sure I spend time with my family and friends. Sometimes I share my troubles with them; other times, I do not. Instead, I enjoy the moments of happiness, talking about everything and nothing. Even in the most stressful times, knowing I have them by my side and can depend on them, makes me feel like I can tackle any of life's challenges. Friends make me happy, and this is not unusual, as many other people take solace in talking to their friends.

The joys of friendships

Research shows that having friends in our lives is so important to our well-being that it can predict our happiness[72]. People who do not have friends are on average less happy than those who do. And that also applies to introverts. Introverts are those of us who enjoy being alone, which is how they often re- charge their energy[73]. My mum is a great example of an introvert. She spends a lot of time by herself and is never bored. Her mind, thoughts, feelings, or other inner-world experiences keep her occupied and happy. She does, however, have one best friend, who she meets every day, and she also makes sure to catch up daily with her sisters to see how they are getting on. What she most enjoys about the people in her life is not being crowded by them, rather the depth of their relationships. After all, it is not the quantity, rather the quality of our friendships that makes us ultimately happier[74].

There are many reasons why friendships are good for us. Firstly, they offer us invaluable support[75]. We know that if we are in trouble, friends are there to pick us up and help us live better lives. It is not even their actions that matter, rather the fact that they are there. They also protect us from loneliness[76]. They are constant witnesses to the comings and goings of our lives, both in the frontline and the background. They keep our lives busy and make us feel less lonely, as we always have things to see and places to go in their valued company.

Personally, what I love about friendships is the intimacy and self-validation they provide[77]. I know that I can discuss with my friends any topics I want; topics that I would not dare to talk about with strangers. I know that no matter what my opinions are, my friends would not judge me. They might not agree with what I say, but appreciate this difference of opinion anyway.

For example, I have a friend who is very different to me. In fact, every time we get each other any birthday or Christmas presents, she always jokes that she buys me something she would not like herself. Despite thinking so differently, and liking so many different things in life, we value our differences, as they make us both more open-minded and offer us a unique view on situations. This is how friends create a safe environment for each other to flourish and be ourselves. Regardless of who we are and what we do, we hear them say: hey, you are perfectly fine, just the way you are.

Support, protection from loneliness, intimacy, and self-validation are just a handful of benefits friendships provide us with. There are over 1,000 academic articles about benefits of friendship. However, the best way to consider the benefits is by thinking back to all our friends and how they contributed to our lives. What did they give you that was priceless? Imagine your life without them. How different would it be? What would you be missing the most without your friends by your side? These are some of the questions that will help you identify the benefits of friendships for you. After all, friendships matter a lot.

Friends and happiness after 30

We know that having friends in our lives is good. The question is, what does this have to do with happiness after 30? It is simple: our network of friends changes throughout our lifespan.

When we are young, we are usually surrounded by friends. By the time we finish secondary school they take up almost 30% of our daily life. This trend continues into our 20s, only to drastically change in our late 30s and early 40s, when we spend barely 7% of our time with friends[78]. Considering how helpful friendships are, is it any wonder that our happiness is affected at around this time?

Approximately 400 people become our friends throughout our lives, but only 10% of the friendships last[79]. Of the 10% who stay our friends, some are very close, others we see less frequently; nonetheless they are still witnesses to our life events and make a difference to our level of happiness.

Making new friends is relatively easy, and technology often helps us do it. We have Meetup (www.meetup.com), where anyone can create or join an interest group that will allow them to make new friends. There, you can find people with whom you can hike, debate, write, read, dance, go sightseeing, visit a museum, have dinner or a drink with, or do whatever else you want to do. Apart from this, we also have social networking sites, online groups, and other organisations that can bring people closer together.

A few years ago, when I moved into my area, I wanted to get to know my neighbours a little bit better. Since I love reading, I wondered if anybody living near me shared my interest in the written word. I put up fliers around my village, knocked at a few people's doors, and posted a notice on the local online community page about a new bookclub looking for members. Soon, 12 of us signed up and this year we are celebrating our 6th anniversary. It is easy to make friends, but more challenging to keep them.

When our lives become busy building a family and a career, it is sometimes hard to keep friendships going. One of my clients, Tim, is in his thirties. He came to me feeling unhappy and dissatisfied with his life. He experienced many symptoms of depression and did not quite know what he could do to turn things around.

He met his wife when they were both in their 20s. They got married, bought a house, and had three beautiful children, one shortly after the other. He loves his family very much and feels guilty about his depression. *How can I be so unhappy, when I have all I have ever wanted?* – he asked me when I met him first.

As I continued to listen to him, one thing became obvious: his children sapped the life out of him and his wife. They were both stuck on a hamster wheel and did not know how to get off it.

Tim used to be a very sociable person. For years, he hung out with a gang of mates he met in college. However, ever since his first child was born, he devoted himself completely to his family, and neglected everyone else in his life. By the time I met him, he had not seen any of his friends for six years. He could not believe it had happened, as it was so gradual. His mates tried to reach out to him, but he was always too busy to respond. Eventually, they stopped calling.

My first challenge for Tim was to rekindle his long-lost friendships. His initial reaction was: *No!* – as he felt embarrassed about not calling them back, and afraid that his mates were not the people they used to be. However, after reflecting upon it, he decided to give it a try. Within two weeks he had meetings arranged with a few of his friends and he could not believe how easy it was. *It is, as if the time had not passed* – he told me afterwards with a big smile on his face.

We worked together for almost two months. During this time Tim's life changed significantly for the better. His depression eased and he began to feel joy and happiness once again. His beloved wife, seeing the change in him, went on her own journey of rekindling her friendships. Soon both felt more balance in their lives whilst their children saw their parents happier and more energised to play with them. It always amazes me how small changes can make huge differences in people's lives.

What happened to Tim and his wife is not unusual for couples with young children. As we get into our 30s, we sometimes forget about our basic needs and fall into the trap of the 30s happiness dip. As we enter our 40s and 50s we are often left with a lower number of friends. It is as if a tornado came through which left our lives stripped to the bare bones. Those who managed to stand by our side in the midst of the storm, we get even closer to. We are more grateful to have them in our lives and the quality of our friendships improve. Sometimes, we manage to rekindle the lost friendships, or make new ones, which may be why as we get through our 40s, our happiness increases.

You are who you spend your time with

When I was doing my PhD, I did some contract work with a client, who insisted that I work in their office for one day a week, over two months. I used to enjoy driving there, having a chat with the girls in the office. The only problem was Kirsty. She was a receptionist and one of the most negative people I have ever met in my life. When something good happened, she somehow managed to turn it into a bad thing. The result was that during our lunch hour, everyone would laugh away, tell stories from their life but only until she walked into the canteen. Her walking in used to change the atmosphere for the worse.

Whether we like it or not, people around us have the power to change our mood and the level of our happiness. Consider people closest to you, your family members, friends whom you spend a lot of time with. When they are happy, chances are that you become happier, too. It may be because they take more time to talk to you, the topics you discuss make you both laugh, or create hopefulness, joy, excitement, and other positive emotions. On the other hand, when they are going through a tough patch, we often become more solemn ourselves. We may reflect upon the unfairness of life, or become worried about them or their circumstances. Either way, fluctuations in happiness of people closest to us has a significant effect on our own happiness.

It is particularly true for middle aged adults [80]. When your friends experience positive events in their lives, such as birth of their children, promotion, holidays, and similar, listening about it, celebrating their successes and, in general, being part of their happiness enhances our own experiences of positivity and reduces our experiences of negativity. We laugh more, joke more, play more, and feel more elated when we see our friends happy.

On the other hand, when they experience negative events, such as health, marital, or financial problems, our emotions change accordingly. What is particularly interesting is that middle aged people were significantly more affected by their friends' events than older participants [81]. In other words, they were happier when their friends were happier, and more miserable when their friends were going through tough times.

Our friends are not the only group of people who significantly alter our happiness. In an ingenious study, psychologists from the University of California and Harvard Medical School collaborated to identify the effect of many different social networks, including friendships, on our happiness [82]. They searched through the scientific data of over 4,000 people who were followed over 20 years, and found that happiness, as well as unhappiness, comes in clusters. When someone in our network becomes less happy, automatically it has a negative effect on other people in our network making the clusters unhappy. Thus, our immediate friends have a 15% impact on our happiness, whilst friends of friends have a 10% impact on us. Interestingly enough, even friends of those friends have a 5.6% impact on us, even though we are not directly associated with them. Moreover, when we are surrounded by happy people, it makes us more likely to be happier in the future. Therefore, we need people in our lives, but we also need to remember that they have the power to impact on our happiness, so let's make wise choices about who we spend our time with.

As we have seen in this chapter, the number of friends we have changes throughout our lifespan. Whilst earlier years are associated with a higher number of friends, our friendships tend to dwindle as we reach midlife. During that stage, we might have less time to give to our friends and less energy to invest into nurturing our friendships. Also, our friends' moods and life circumstances have an influence on us. Therefore, if they go through a dip in their happiness around their 30s and 40s, chances are we will feel less happy, too. All this makes it more likely for our happiness to drop around midlife.

Once we pass through the tough times, we might be left with a lower number of friends by our side, but the quality of our friendships might be better. By then, we have gone through a lot together and developed skills that allow us to keep our relationship growing. At this stage, it is not the number of friends that matters, rather knowing that the selected ones are there, ready to help us when we need them. Conversely, we are there for them, ready to offer support when required. That knowledge makes a big difference to our lives, as it fulfils our need for belonging. All these changes may be the reason why we feel happier as we age.

THE HILLS AND MOUNTAINS OF LIFE

Life is hard and then you die – this is what James used to say to Harry in a major TV show called *Dempsey and Makepeace.* It was one of my favourite programmes in the 1980s, and founded the beginning of my life-long love for detective stories, which makes me stay up late at night watching Hercule Poirot, the White Collar, and other TV shows. As gloomy as the above motto sounds, I was very impressionable as a teenager, so it stayed with me for life. Over the years, I have adjusted it to my own, less cynical and more cheerful version: *Life is short and then you die*, which encourages me to live my life to the full. However, what I lost out on by tweaking it, is the essence of what James meant, which is that life is not a flat terrain, rather a hilly landscape, which sometimes turns into mountains that can be challenging to conquer.

One researcher, desperate to figure out the reasons for U-shaped happiness, analysed data from thousands of participants in the British Household

Panel Survey[83]. He considered many explanations for variations in people's life satisfaction. He examined differences in gender, race, educational level, and many other variables. What he found was that life events seemed to have significant influence on our well-being changes. When analysing participants' responses, as soon as he took life events out of the equation, the U-shaped happiness became a straight line without any dips around the age of 30 or 40.

This makes a lot of sense, as after all, our life circumstances have an impact on our well-being. Let us take having children, as an example. Research shows that the birth of a child is associated with sudden, small to medium deterioration in the marital satisfaction of new parents[84]. They no longer have time for each other, put less effort into building their relationship and more effort into being the best mums and dads they can. This decline continues up until the child reaches the age of seven, at which stage it stabilises and not-so-new anymore parents' marital satisfaction begins to improve. At the same time, married individuals who are not parents, do not experience the same decline in their relationship satisfaction, which suggests that indeed, our life events, such as having a child, can affect our levels of well-being quite significantly.

So, what events can potentially influence happiness changes? Can we predict them? Well, partially we can. After all, the clear majority of us follow a typical life-journey pattern. We go to school and possibly to college or University, then work, we meet someone we choose to spend our lives with, buy a home, have children, then grandchildren arrive and we spend the winter of our lives either with our family by our side, or in an old folks' home. Even people whose lives are atypical tend to follow a similar developmental journey based on fulfilling their needs of intimacy (surrounding themselves with friends), finding a meaningful career, and spending time contributing to the growth and life improvement of the next generation[85]. These developmental stages make us ultimately more fulfilled in life.

As all these events occur, they affect our feelings and how satisfied we are with our lives. Some researchers claim that our circumstances influence our happiness by only 10%[86]. However, considering that life events straighten up the U-shaped happiness dip, it is possible that our circumstances may impact our happiness more significantly than that. In order to illustrate this impact, let us look at both the mountain and hilly terrain of our existence; in other words, traumas and daily life stressors.

The mountain terrain

Traumas are sudden events in our lives that allow us to pinpoint clearly the times before and after the event[87]. They may include the death of someone close to us, being made redundant, or an unexpected accident. We can clearly see what our lives were like before it happened, and how this event has changed them.

Research shows that we experience, on average, about one *potentially* traumatic event in our lives[88]. It is potentially traumatic, as not everyone is significantly affected by it. What makes me upset might not be upsetting to you. This is why, it is a *potentially* traumatic, not necessarily a traumatic event.

One of my potentially traumatic events was the car crash I mentioned earlier. As I slammed on my breaks, my car began to aquaplane making me temporarily lose control over it. After the accident, as I was waiting for the towing truck to arrive, I sat on the side of the road wondering what I could have done differently. *Could I have prevented this accident from happening? Perhaps if I had changed my tyres, they would have gripped the road better, thus preventing my car from aquaplaning. If only I could predict traumatic events, perhaps I might also be able to prevent accidents* – I thought. Well, perhaps we can.

According to research, when we are aged between 35 and 44, our odds of experiencing traumatic events in life are greater than when we are aged 15-24 or 45-54[89]. This could be because we are already less happy around this time of our lives, therefore, our concentration may be impaired making us more prone to accidents. Or, it could be because there is so much happening in our lives that our chances of experiencing trauma are increased. After all, if we did not have to drop the kids to that birthday party, we would not have been on that road, and would not have crashed that car. Having a party to go to created an opportunity for a traumatic event to happen. Also, let us not forget that midlife is often the time when we experience our first serious loss in life. Our parents pass away and we are left trying to make sense of other people's and our own mortality. All this may contribute to experiencing potentially traumatic events in midlife.

Regardless of the reasons for the greater prevalence of traumatic events in our late 30s and early 40s, it oddly coincides with a dip in our happiness. Most of us are resilient and can cope with traumatic events effectively[90]. However, regardless of how well we cope, they can still take a lot out of us. Even when we report psychological growth after a traumatic event, it is often entangled with some symptoms of depression, such as negative thoughts, negative feelings, or temporary insomnia[91]. Traumatic events drain us and make our lives more challenging, thus lowering our satisfaction and overall well-being, which may be one of the reasons for a dip in our midlife. However, traumas are not the only reason for lesser happiness, as the hilly terrain can be very challenging, too.

The hilly terrain

What is more detrimental to our health: daily life stresses or big traumatic events? Is it the stress of having to get up for work every day, battle our way through traffic, the ever-expanding length of our to-do list, the laptop not working as swiftly as we would like it to (do not even mention the Wi-Fi!), coping with our children's random outbursts, cooking the same dinner for the umpteenth time, and bickering with our partner before going to bed? Or are traumatic events, such as the death of someone close to us, more detrimental to our health?

Research shows that it is the small, nagging, ever-lasting daily stresses that have a more negative effect on our physical[92] and psychological[93] well- being, much more so than larger events. When something big and nasty occurs in our lives it is very easy to understand why it makes us feel bad, and as a result we give ourselves a break. We know we are going through a tough patch, so even if we behave out of character, we forgive ourselves for the outburst. We realise that someday the pain will ease and we will feel better again. More importantly, when we deal with a major life event, we receive significantly more help from people around us. At work, our manager asks us to take it easy for a while; at home our family and friends make sure we are not on our own, even the neighbours pitch in and drop off a lovely, home-made lasagne to ease our lives; and sometimes we might even want to reach out to a counsellor to help us through this difficult period of our lives. As challenging as the big and negative events are, we somehow find a way to cope with them and adjust.

One of my clients, Sean, was barely able to keep his head above water when he was in his early 40s. He had a big job with a multitude of daily duties, a big house to pay for, and a big family to look after. All in all, his life was big and sometimes he found it overwhelming. Then, one day a tragedy occurred. He went to the doctor with persistent headache and within a week, after an array of tests, he was diagnosed with a rare eye degeneration disorder and told that he would lose his sight over the next three years. The shock of the diagnosis made him stop and re-consider his life choices. As traumatic as it was, it helped him grow through his adversity, change his life direction, and most importantly, slow down. Once he slowed down, his daily hassles decreased making his life more manageable. I met him seven years later. He still had his eyesight, and owed it to the new pace of life.

Big life events are like the mountains we climb. We summon all our energy to reach the top. We know it is going to be tough, so we get all our mountain gear ready, get the right shoes, and go. It is different with daily hassles. They are like small hills to climb. We might not even consciously notice that we are climbing up the hill, but after a while we feel it in our bones.

The problem with daily hassles is that they are at us every day; even when we try to deal with major life events, they are there to nag at us all of the time. If we imagine our life as a path across a large field with space behind us and in front of us, they are like the crops we see around us, never-ending. We know other people have to deal with similarly small issues in their daily lives, so we do not even bother telling them about ours, and continue to suffer in silence.

We see others smiling, joking, and seemingly coping well with daily stresses every day, and rather than feeling inspired by their strength, we look at ourselves even more critically wondering what is wrong with us for not being able to cope with ours. This may be why daily hassles can make us feel worse about ourselves than traumatic life events.

Some researchers show that midlife is not only associated with more traumatic events in our lives, but also a greater number of smaller, nagging stressors[94]. They pile up on top of each other making it so much more difficult to deal with them. We are wondering how to pay our next mortgage repayment, buy that Xbox game for our son, find the time to tidy up the house before the in-laws arrive, negotiate with our client at work, and figure out a way to eat that soggy sandwich amid it all. The problem with all these dilemmas is that they happen to us all at the same time. The more we juggle, the less likely we are to resolve our issues, making us feel exhausted and deeming our problems unsurmountable.

The good news is that as we move from mid- into later life, our daily stressors decrease in volume[95]. We begin to resolve all the unresolved issues. The firefighting we experience in our 30s and 40s may leave us a little shaken up. However, as we progress into our 50s, and all the hassles slowly begin to decrease, we have more time, better developed skills, and can put more effort into fixing our unresolved issues, and rebuilding our lives in whatever way we want. This could be the reason as to why life gets happier with age.

In the meantime, there is not much we can do about experiencing these stressful life events. The trick is not to think that they will last forever. As they keep happening to us, it may feel like they are never-ending. One shot after the next keeps knocking us down to our knees. Then, when we least expect it, we get another shove, fall down, and find it hard to summon the energy to get up again. When life treats you badly, just remember it is usually transient. Just like clouds in the sky, life stressors will pass and we will soon feel better again.

WHEN IT ALL STARTS TO MAKE SENSE

Imagine that you live in a world that you can well predict. You know that when you smile to strangers, they will usually smile back at you. If they do not it may have nothing to do with you, rather what they are pondering about in their head. You know that when bad things happen in your life you will soon find many ways to deal with them effectively. You know that most of the time you can guess what winds other people up, thus are able to single-handedly prevent tricky situations from happening. Imagine that your knowledge of the world can help you predict other people's actions, and that you can do what is necessary, well in advance, to keep the people you love safe from danger. Imagine how much more comfortable your life would feel like if it were like this. The good news is that you do not need to imagine it for too long, because our lives become more predictable as we age[96].

The most rapid increase in the way we can predict our world happens when we are in our 20s. We experience tricky life situations and despite not having any experience in dealing with them, we somehow find a solution to our problems, which allows us to develop our wisdom and helps us feel more confident about our lives[97]. Our psychological, social, and intellectual resources continue to grow and soon, our world becomes a more structured entity to tackle and it begins to make more sense, in other words, we are able to predict the implications of people's actions better.

As we move into our 30s, we have a well-developed sense of predictability, however, given the busy times we are embarking upon, this comprehension begins to plateau. We experience a whole array of new life situations that curb our initial development of such predictability and perhaps make us doubt some of our previously created rules of the world.

One of my friends has always believed in the kindness of people. She trusted in our good intentions and was almost naïve in her views. She always used to say that life is hard enough for us all, so we should help, not hinder each other. Her optimism about humankind has been touching, and allowed her to behave in ways that usually elicited goodness in others, from whom we might not have expected it, until one day when she let two strangers into her home. They tied her up, stole her belongings and left her shaken up physically and mentally for a long time. Her belief in the goodness of people underwent a testing period, and she began to doubt her initial believes about the world. Soon, nonetheless, she readjusted her views and today she continues to trust that most people are good. At the same there are some who are not, so we need to be careful who we trust.

These types of adjustments in beliefs can happen at any stage of our lives. However, whilst we are in our 30s and 40s we might be exposed to more new and challenging events that test our previously set rules of the world. This could be the reason as to why our predictability of the world stabilises around this time and we do not experience as much growth in it as we had up to the age of 30. According to research, between the ages of 30 and 45 we report only small increases in the way we view our world as predictable, comprehensible, and structured. For most of us, a slight confusion may set in as we adjust our beliefs[98].

Then, as of the age of 45, our predictability of the world begins to grow more steadily again all the way until the age of 85, showing the highest levels in the winter of our lives. Such predictability makes us feel like we are more in control of our lives and our environment. We can make more informed decisions about our lives and sit in the driver seat of our life journey. This may be yet another reason why our happiness grows in later life.

THE BOAT WITH A PURRING ENGINE

When younger and older people are asked about their views about happiness changes across their lifespan, both groups believe that being older is associated with decreases in happiness [99]. Older people reckon that they are less happy than their younger counterparts, and predict that their happiness will continue to decline as they age. Yet, when people of all ages are asked to complete psychological questionnaires to assess levels of well-being, we systematically show increases of happiness and decreases of depression as we move from the summer, through to the autumn and winter of our lives. This misprediction of our well-being can become a self-fulfilling prophecy making us feel worse as we age. I hope that this book has helped you look at it slightly differently.

Over the last few chapters, you have read about what I believe are the five reasons as to why our happiness increases after the initial 30s and 40s dip. As we age, we learn to adjust to the shrinking future by focusing more on the good old times. This in turn, allows us to savour the events in our lives and make us feel like we have had a valuable and worthwhile existence that is full of meaning and purpose.

Year by year, as we learn how to manage our emotions, our lives become more stable and free from extreme ups and downs. It takes us longer to get upset, as we choose to notice the positive aspects of our lives and experience more positive emotions. Furthermore, as we age, we develop the ability to sustain this positivity, which ultimately brings more happiness into our later years and makes them more enjoyable.

As our emotional stability grows, so too does the quality of our social networks. After all, it is easier to be around people whose emotions are not too extreme. In later life, we may have less friends than we had before, but the ones that are left by our side are usually people who we trust a lot, and with whom we truly enjoy spending our time. After we retire, we also have more time to dedicate to them, which allows us to develop our friendships further, enhancing our sense of belonging and making us ultimately happier.

The increase in our free time is also connected with our lives becoming less hectic. Whilst our midlife has us running around in circles trying to deal with a multitude of adversities all at the same time, later life stages are associated with a smaller volume of stressors. They are still there but are not as frequent as they used to be. Also, we have learnt how to resolve them, which is why we might not spend too much time worrying about them. This may have a more positive impact on our well-being.

Progress through our lives is associated with learning. As we observe daily life situations unfolding, we learn to predict other people's and our own reactions to them. Next time, when a similar situation happens, we adjust our behaviour and hopefully get a better result. This predictability helps us build a sense of mastery that we have over our environment. We know that no matter what happens, we can always find ways to cope with life challenges. This could be one other reason as to why our lives become significantly more balanced and comprehensible as we grow older, which leaves us with a feeling of empowerment.

These five reasons for our happiness increasing later on in life are not exhaustive. Psychological literature offers several other explanations for the potential increase of happiness. For example, as we age, we become more resilient and can see the world beyond our own concerns [100]. Becoming less self-centred can help us notice that other people are worse off than us, thus instead of feeling self-pity, we may experience heightened levels of gratitude.

Also, as we age, we are more able to come to terms with our life longings[101]. For years, we may have longed to become someone (a pilot, winner of The X Factor, a famous actor) or do something else (return to education, go travelling, do pottery). This was a goal we tried to achieve throughout our lives, but for whatever reason, we did not manage to. Then, as we began to realise that we do not have enough time or skills, or we simply choose not to pursue it further, our goal becomes a life longing, which is easier to manage. Life longing is a coping strategy for unfulfilled goals. It allows us to accept that certain things will never happen, but it is ok, as our lives continue to go on.

These and other processes take place inside us discretely as we age. Because they happen so gradually we adjust to them as we go along and often do not notice how we change. It is like we are on this boat with a well-oiled purring engine that does not distract us with rapid movements or sudden noise. We slowly travel through our life time gathering experiences and adjusting our course. Before we notice, we find ourselves in a different place and by then we advance skills to steer the boat proficiently and develop different needs and wants that are important in our lives. We may no longer care about extra wrinkles[102] on our face or the fact that our memory is not as good as it used to be[103]. Instead we learn to value our knowledge and life experiences which make us the people we are. This process of acceptance allows us to live a better life as we age.

SURFING THE WAVES

That day when I attended a lecture by the guest lecturer from Harvard changed my life. Years of reading about Positive Psychology, happiness, well-being, and specifically about the evidence of U-shaped happiness made me realise that I do not have to try so hard to be happier.

Previously, when I was not feeling well, I blamed myself for it. If only I did more of this, or less of that – I used to think – I'd feel so much better now. Nowadays, I just roll with it When I am not having a good day, I let it run its course. Often, by the evening I begin to laugh at my lack of luck. It is funny how sometimes things go from bad to worse in a short space of time. It is even funnier how they turn around just as quickly. And sometimes all we need to do is just weather the storm.

I like to view it as surfing the waves of negativity. When I am having a bad day, it is like I am facing this enormous wave that overwhelms me. I do not give up easily, so initially I give my very best to try and change its course. I chat with my partner, friends, and family, write my thoughts in my diary, go to the gym or for a walk to get some exercise, count my blessings, and do all the other things I know that usually help. Sometimes they get me out of trouble, other times they do not. When the waves of negativity are still overwhelming, I imagine grabbing a surf board, lying down on it, watching out for the best time to stand up, and then enjoy surfing on the waves of negativity. Once I let go and accept that it is just the time I am going through, things usually become easier. Before I notice, I get out of the stormy waters, and have tales to tell that keep making me psychologically stronger.

Surfing the waves is not about giving up. It is about knowing when to stop fighting, embracing what is happening to us at this moment in time, and learning from these experiences, so that we do not make the same mistakes again. Rather than wanting the waters to be still, thinking how much better it would be to be elsewhere, or exerting our energy beating ourselves up, it is about accepting that we are where we are, and all we can do is just get on that surf board and hope it takes us to a better place. This is all we can control at the moment.

Just because happiness seems U-shaped does not mean that we will experience only one dip in our lives. Adversities happen and they will continue to happen, but the way we deal with them is going to be different as we learn new skills and knowledge after 30. Conversely, we will continue making mistakes, because to err is human. However, as we grow older, we will deal with these mistakes differently and they will not upset us as much. After all, research says that moderate adversities in life make us ultimately happier than experiencing no adversities at all[104].

If you are going through a difficult year, or perhaps the last several years have been tough, just keep reminding yourself that it is temporary. The same way as things change for the worse, they can also change for the better. Aim every day to get the best out of the stormy times. Stormy times, which are the bottom part of U-shaped happiness, are not bad times, they are simply times we pass through.

My cousin is a photographer. She takes some amazing pictures. One of them, black and white, hangs on the main wall of her sitting room. It shows an old, empty pier in the middle of a storm. The waves go up so high, they stand at double the height of the construction. Every time I look at it, it makes me feel humble, scared, but also hopeful and amazed by the beauty of nature. It has been years since she took the photograph, yet the pier continues to stand despite the many storms it weathered. So can we.

My 30s were challenging at times. Now that

I am passed them, I find myself in calmer waters and coping with tricky situations better every day. Each struggle, obstacle, and tear taught me different ways to view my life. I learnt new skills that helped me adapt to my changing circumstances. If I were yanked out of my 20s into my 40s, and skipped a decade, my happiness would have taken a different trajectory. As it stands, however, each year, month, and day taught me invaluable lessons that allowed me to become the person I am today.

As we age, we continue to learn, master our skills, and adapt to changes in our lives. It is a vibrant process that allows us to feel more comfortable in our own skin, in control, and confident about ourselves. It is also a process that makes us ultimately happier in the autumn and winter of our lives. All we need to do is trust it fully, and when things get tough, hope that tomorrow we are one day closer to better times.

References

1. Norcross, J. C. (2000) Here comes the self-help revolution in mental health. Psychotherapy: Theory, Research, Practice, Training, 37: 370-377.

2. Starker, S. (2002) Oracle at the Supermarket: The American Preoccupation with Self-help Books. New Brunswick: Transaction Publishers.

3. Neville, P. (2012) Helping self-help books: Working towards a new research agenda. Interactions: Studies in Communication & Culture, 3: 361-379.

4. Nehring, D., Alvarado, E., Hendricks, E., & Kerrigan, D. (2016) Transnational Popular Psychology and Global Self-help Industry: The Politics of Contemporary Social Change. Basingstoke, Hampshire: Palgarve MacMillan.

5. 5 Travelex. (2009) Re-FUN-dancy: Recession fuels growth of grown up gapper.
London, England: Author. Retrieved from http://www. travelex.co.uk/press/
ENG/doc-recession-fuels-growth-of-grown-up-gapper. asp

6. Seligman, M. P., Steen, T. A., Park, N. and Peterson, C. (2005) Positive psychology progress: Empirical validation of interventions. American Psychologist, 60: 410-421.

7. 7 Mitchell, J., Vella-Brodrick, D. and Klein, B., (2010) Positive psychology and the internet: A mental Health

Opportunity. Electronic Journal of Applied Psychology, 6: 30-41.

8.   8 Mauss, I. B., Savino, N. S., Anderson, C. L., Weisbuch, M., Tamir, M. and Laudenslager, M. L. (2012) The pursuit of happiness can be lonely. Emotion, 12: 908-912; Mauss, I. B., Tamir, M., Anderson, C. L. and Savino, N. S. (2011) Can seeking happiness make people unhappy? Paradoxical effects of valuing happiness. Emotion, 11: 807-815.

9.   Lawrence, B. S. (1980) The Myth of the Midlife Crisis. Sloan Management Review, 21: 35-49.

10. Blanchflower, D. G. and Oswald, A. J. (2008) Is well-being U-shaped over the life cycle?. Social Science & Medicine, 66: 1733-1749.

11. Blanchflower and Oswald (ibid.)

12. Clark, A. E. and Oswald, A. J. (2006) The curved relationship between subjective well-being and age. PARIS-Jourdan Sciences Economiques, working paper no. 29.

13. E.g. Williams, B., & Harter, S. (2010) Views of the self and others at different ages: utility of repertory grid technique in detecting the positivity effect in aging. International Journal of Aging & Human Development, 71: 1-22; Westerhof, G. and Keyes, C. (2010) Mental illness and mental health: The two Continua Model across the lifespan. Journal of Adult Development, 17: 110-119. – showed u-shaped happiness for emotional well-being,

but decline for older adults in psychological well-being.

14. Tov, W. and Au, E. M. (2013) Comparing well-being across nations: Conceptual and empirical issues. In S. A. David, I. Boniwell, A. Conley Ayers, S. A. David, I. Boniwell and A. Conley Ayers (Eds.), The Oxford handbook of happiness (pp. 449-464). New York, NY, US: Oxford University Press.

15. Drassinover, A. (2003) Freud's Theory of Culture: Eros, Loss, and Politics. Oxford, UK: Rowman & Littlefield Publishers, Inc.

16. Diener, E. and Biswas-Diener, R. (2008). Happiness: Unlocking the Mysteries of Psychological Wealth. Malden, MA: Blackwell Publishing.

17. Frijters, P. and Beatton, T. (2012) The mystery of the U-shaped relationship between happiness and age. Journal of Economic Behavior and Organization, 82: 525–542.

18. Hefferon, K. (2013). Positive Psychology and the Body: The Somatopsychic Side to Flourishing. Maidenhead, UK: Open University Press.

19. Ryff, C. D. (2013) Psychological well-being revisited: Advances in the science and practice of eudaimonia. Psychotherapy & Psychosomatics, 83: 10-28.

20. Hefferon, K. and Boniwell, I. (2011) Positive psychology: Theory, Research and Applications. Maidenhead: Open University Press.

21. Ryff (ibid.)

22. Ryff, C. D. and Essex, M. J. (1992) The interpretation of life experience and well-being: The sample case of relocation. Psychology and Aging, 7: 507-517.

23. Ward, M. C. (2001) Life-span contextualism and life acceptance in self narrative: Adult understanding of the mother-daughter relationship. Dissertation Abstracts International, North Caroline State University.

24. Rath, T. and Harter, J. (2010) Well-being: The Five Essential Elements. New York: Gallup Press.

25. Aked, J., Marks, N., Cordon, C. and Thompson, C. (2008) Five Ways to Wellbeing. London: New Economics Foundation.

26. Hefferon (ibid.)

27. Seligman, M.E.P. (2011) Flourish: A New Understanding of Happiness and Well-being – and How to Achieve Them. London: Nicholas Brealey Publishing.

28. Burke, J. & Minton, S.J. (2016) Re-thinking well-being: Deficit vs. strength approach in measuring the impact of bullying and cyberbullying in schools. In L. Corcoran & C. Mc Guckin (Eds.) Bullying and Cyberbullying: Prevalence, psychological impacts, and intervention strategies. New York: Nova.

29. Keyes, C. M. (2005) Mental illness and/or mental health? Investigating axioms of the complete state model of health. Journal of Consulting & Clinical Psychology, 73: 539-548.

30. Huppert, F. and Whittington, J. (2003) Evidence for the

independence of positive and negative well-being: Implications for quality of life assessment. British Journal of Health Psychology, 8: 107-122.

31. Fredrickson, B. L., Tugade, M. M., Waugh, C. E., & Larkin, G. R. (2003). What Good Are Positive Emotions in Crises? A Prospective Study of Resilience and Emotions Following the Terrorist Attacks on the United States on September 11th, 2001. Journal of Personality & Social Psychology, 84: 365-376.

32. Blanchflower, D. G. and Oswald, A. J. (2008) Is well-being U-shaped over the life cycle? Social Science & Medicine, 66: 1733-1749.

33. Blanchflower, D. G., & Oswald, A. J. (2016). Antidepressants and age: A new form of evidence for U-shaped well-being through life. Journal of Economic Behavior & Organization, 127: 46-58.

34. Zimbardo, P. and Boyd, J. (2008) The Time Paradox: The New Psychology of Time That Will Change Your Life. New York, NY, US: Free Press.

35. Schechter, D. and Francis, C. (2010) A life history approach to understanding youth time preference. Human Nature, 21: 140-164.

36. Chen, P. and Vazsonyi, A. T. (2011) Future orientation, impulsivity, and problem behaviors: A longitudinal moderation model. Developmental Psychology, 47: 1633-1645.

37. Zimbardo and Boyd (ibid.)

38. Zimbardo and Boyd (ibid.)

39. Zimbardo and Boyd (ibid.)

40. Brothers, A., Chui, H. and Diehl, M. (2014) Measuring future time perspective across adulthood: Development and evaluation of a brief multidimensional questionnaire. The Gerontologist, 54: 1075-1088.

41. Cheng, S. and Yim, Y. (2008) Age differences in forgiveness: The role of future time perspective. Psychology and Aging, 23: 676-680.

42. Bono, G., McCullough, M.E. and Root, L.M. (2008) Forgiveness, feeling connected to others, and well-being: Two longitudinal studies. Personality and Social Psychology Bulletin, 34: 182-195.

43. Witvliet van Oyen, C., Ludwig, T.E. and Laan, K.L.V. (2001) Granting forgiveness or harboring grudges: Implications for emotion, physiology and health. American Psychological Society, 12: 117-123.

44. Cheng and Yim (ibid.)

45. Sword, R. M., Sword, R. M., Brunskill, S. R. and Zimbardo, P. G. (2014) Time Perspective Therapy: A new time-based Metaphor Therapy for PTSD. Journal of Loss & Trauma, 19: 197-201.

46. Boniwell, I. and Zimbardo, P. (2003) Time to find the right balance. The Psychologist, 16: 129-131.

47. Zimbardo and Boyd (ibid.)

48. Zambianchi, M. (2015) Time perspective and psychological well-being in old age. Applied

Psychology Bulletin, 63: 3-14.

49. Boniwell and Zimbardo (ibid.)

50. Zimbardo and Boyd (ibid.)

51. Vaillant, G. E. (2007) Aging well. The American Journal of Geriatric Psychiatry, 15: 181-183.

52. Charles, S., Mather, M. and Carstensen, L. L. (2003) Aging and emotional memory: The forgettable nature of negative images for older adults. Journal of Experimental Psychology: General, 132: 310-324.

53. Fredrickson, B. (2009) Positivity: Groundbreaking Research Reveals How to Embrace the Hidden Strength of Positive Emotions, Overcome Negativity, and Thrive. New York, NY, US: Crown Publishers/Random House.

54. Bahrami, F., Kasaei, R. and Zamani, A. (2012) Preventing worry and rumination by induced positive emotion. International Journal of Preventive Medicine, 3: 102-109.

55. Moskowitz, J. T. (2001) Emotion and coping. In T. J. Mayne, G. A. Bonanno, T. J. Mayne, G. A. Bonanno (Eds.), Emotions: Current issues and future directions (pp. 311-336). New York, NY, US: Guilford Press.

56. Charles, S. T., Piazza, J. R., Gloria, L. and Almeida, D. M. (2009) Now you see it, now you don't: Age differences in affective reactivity to social tensions. Psychology & Aging, 24: 645-653.

57. Charles, S. T., & Almeida, D. M. (2006) Daily reports of symptoms and negative affect: Not all symptoms are the same. Psychology & Health, 21: 1-17.

58. Carstensen, L. L., Turan, B., Scheibe, S., Ram, N., Ersner-Hershfield, H., Samanez-Larkin, G. R. and Nesselroade, J. R. (2011) Emotional experience improves with age: Evidence based on over 10 years of experience sampling. Psychology and Aging, 26: 21–33.

59. Positivity Ration website: http://www.positivityratio.com/single.php

60. Fredrickson, B. L. and Losada, M. F. (2005) Positive affect and the complex dynamics of human flourishing. American Psychologist, 60: 678-686.

61. Brown, N. J. L., Sokal, A. D. and Friedman, H. L. (2013) The complex dynamics of wishful thinking: The critical positivity ratio. American Psychologist, 68: 801–813.

62. Fredrickson, B. L. and Losada, M. F. (2013) Positive affect and the complex dynamics of human flourishing: Correction to Fredrickson and Losada (2005). American Psychologist, 68: 822.

63. Fredrickson, B. L. (2013) Updated thinking on positivity ratios. American Psychologist, 68: 814–822.

64. Diehl, M., Hay, E. L. and Berg, K. M. (2011) The ratio between positive and negative affect and flourishing mental health across adulthood. Aging & Mental Health, 15: 882-893.

65. Linley, P. A., Dovey, H., Beaumont, S., Wilkinson, J. and Hurling, R. (2016) Examining the intensity and frequency of experience of discrete positive emotions. Journal of Happiness Studies, 17: 875-892.

66. Fredrickson, 2009 (ibid.)

67. Schneider, S. and Stone, A. A. (2015) Mixed emotions across the adult life span in the United States. Psychology and Aging, 30: 369-382.

68. Scheibe, S., Freund, A. M. and Baltes, P. B. (2007) Toward a Developmental Psychology of Sehnsucht (Life Longings): The Optimal (Utopian) Life. Developmental Psychology, 43: 778-795.

69. Scheibe, S., Kunzmann, U. and Baltes, P. B. (2009) New territories of positive life-span development: Wisdom and life longings. In S. J. Lopez, C. R. Snyder, S. J. Lopez, C. R. Snyder (Eds.), Oxford handbook of positive psychology, 2nd ed. (pp. 171-183). New York, NY, US: Oxford University Press.

70. Vaillant (ibid.)

71. Folkman, S., Lazarus, R. S., Pimley, S. and Novacek, J. (1987) Age differences in stress and coping processes. Psychology and Aging, 2: 171-184.

72. Myers, D. (2000) The funds, friends and faith of happy people. The American Psychologist, 55: 56–67.

73. Cain, S. (2012) Quiet: The power of introverts in a world that can't stop talking. New York, NY, US: Crown Publishers/Random House.

74. Demir, M. and Weitekamp, L. A. (2007) I am so happy 'cause today I found my friend: Friendship and personality as predictors of happiness. Journal of Happiness Studies, 8: 181–211.

75. Gladow, N. W. and Ray, M. P. (1986) The impact of informal support systems on the well-being of low income single parents. Family Relations: Journal of Applied Family and Child Studies, 35: 113–123.

76. Green, L. R., Richardson, D. S. and Lago, T. (2001) Network correlates of social and emotional loneliness in young and older adults. Personality & Social Psychology Bulletin, 27: 281-288.

77. Cutrona, C., Russell, D. and Rose, J. (1986) Social support and adaptation to stress by the elderly. Psychology and Aging, 1: 47-54.

78. Larson, R. W. and Bradney, N. (1988) Precious moments with family members and friends. In R. M. Milardo, R. M. Milardo (Eds.), Families and social networks (pp. 107-126). Thousand Oaks, CA, US: Sage Publications, Inc.

79. Hoggard, L. (2005) How to be happy. London: BBC Books.

80. Russell, A., Bergeman, C. S. and Scott, S. B. (2012) Daily Social Exchanges and Affect in Middle and Later Adulthood: The Impact of Loneliness and Age. International Journal of Aging & Human Development, 74: 299-329.

81. Ibid.

82. Fowler, J. and Christakis, N. (2009) Dynamic spread of happiness in a large social network: longitudinal analysis of the Framingham Heart Study social network. British Medical Journal (Overseas & Retired Doctors

Edition), 338: 23-27.

83. Movshuk, O. (2011) Why is life satisfaction U-shaped in age? Journal of Behavioral Economics and Finance, 4: 133-138.

84. Doss, B. D., Rhoades, G. K., Stanley, S. M. and Markman, H. J. (2009) The Effect of the transition to parenthood on relationship quality: An 8-Year prospective study. Journal of Personality & Social Psychology, 96(3), 601-619.; Keizer, R., & Schenk, N. (2012) Becoming a parent and relationship satisfaction: A longitudinal dyadic perspective. Journal of Marriage & Family, 74: 759-773.

85. Vaillant (ibid.)

86. Lyubomirsky, S. (2007) The how of happiness: A scientific approach to getting the life you want. New York, NY, US: Penguin Press.

87. Hefferon and Boniwell (ibid.)

88. Bonanno, G. A., & Mancini, A. D. (2008) The human capacity to thrive in the face of potential trauma. Pediatrics, 121: 369-375.

89. Kessler, R. C., Foster, C. L., Saunders, W. B. and Stang, P. E. (1995) Social consequences of psychiatric disorders. American Journal of Psychiatry, 152: 1026-1032.

90. Hefferon and Boniwell (ibid.)

91. Joseph, S. (2011) What doesn't kill us: The new psychology of posttraumatic growth. New York, NY, US: Basic Books.

92. DeLongis, A., Coyne, J. C., Dakof, G., Folkman, S. and

Lazarus, R. S. (1982) Relationship of daily hassles, uplifts, and major life events to health status. Health Psychology, 1: 119-136.

93. Landreville, P. and Vézina, J. (1992) A comparison between daily hassles and major life events as correlates of well-being in older adults. Canadian Journal on Aging, 11: 137-149.

94. Aldwin, C. M., Sutton, K. J., Chiara, G. and Spiro, A. (1996) Age differences in stress, coping, and appraisal: Findings from the Normative Aging Study. Journals of Gerontology: Psychological Sciences, 51: 179–188.

95. Ibid.

96. Nilsson, K. W., Leppert, J., Simonsson, B. and Starrin, B. (2010). Sense of coherence and psychological well-being: Improvement with age. Journal of Epidemiology and Community Health, 64: 347-352.

97. Sagy, S., Antonovsky, A. and Adler, I. (1990) Explaining life satisfaction in later life: The sense of coherence model and activity theory. Behavior, Health, & Aging, 1: 11-25.

98. Nilsson et al. (ibid.)

99. Lacey, H. P., Smith, D. M. and Ubel, P. A. (2006). Hope I die before I get old: Mispredicting happiness across the adult lifespan. Journal of Happiness Studies, 7: 167-182.

100. van Kessel, G. (2013) The ability of older people to overcome adversity: A review of the resilience concept. Geriatric Nursing, 34: 122-127.

101. Mayser, S., Scheibe, S. and Riediger, M. (2008) (Un)reachable? An empirical differentiation of goals and life longings. European Psychologist, 13: 126-140.

102. Clarke, L. H. and Griffin, M. (2007) The body natural and the body unnatural: Beauty work and aging. Journal of Aging Studies, 21: 187-201.

103. Siedlecki, K. L., Donnay, S. M. and Paggi, M. E. (2012) Do values placed on cognitive abilities shift with age? Journal of Positive Psychology, 7: 144-154.

104. Seery, M.D., Holman, E.A. and Silver, R.C. (2010) Whatever does not kill us: Cumulative lifetime adversity, vulnerability, and resilience. Journal of Personality and Social Psychology, 99: 1025-1041.

www.ingramcontent.com/pod-product-compliance
Lightning Source LLC
Chambersburg PA
CBHW031554040426
42452CB00006B/301